Driver & Vehicle
Standards
Agency

The **OFFICIAL DVSA GUIDE** to

RIDING

the essential skills

London: TSO

D1589064

Written and compiled by Driver and Vehicle Standards Agency Learning Materials.

© Crown copyright 2016

First published as *Motorcycle Riding – the essential skills* 1991

New title – *The Official DSA Guide to Riding – the essential skills* 2005
Third edition Crown copyright 2016

ISBN 978 0 11 553414 0

A CIP catalogue record for this book is available from the British Library

Other titles in the Driving Skills series

The Official DVSA Theory Test for Motorcyclists
The Official DVSA Theory Test for Motorcyclists (DVD-ROM)
The Official DVSA Guide to Learning to Ride
Better Biking – the official DVSA training aid (DVD)

The Official DVSA Theory Test Kit iPhone App
The Official DVSA Highway Code iPhone App
The Official DVSA Hazard Perception Practice iOS App

The Official DVSA Guide to Driving – the essential skills
The Official DVSA Theory Test for Car Drivers
The Official DVSA Theory Test for Car Drivers (DVD-ROM)
The Official DVSA Guide to Learning to Drive
Prepare for your Practical Driving Test (DVD)
The Official DVSA Highway Code Interactive CD-ROM
The Official DVSA Guide to Hazard Perception (DVD-ROM)

The Official DVSA Guide to Driving Buses and Coaches
The Official DVSA Guide to Driving Goods Vehicles
The Official DVSA Theory Test for Drivers of Large Vehicles
The Official DVSA Theory Test for Drivers of Large Vehicles (DVD-ROM)
Driver CPC – the official DVSA guide for professional bus and coach drivers
Driver CPC – the official DVSA guide for professional goods vehicle drivers

The Official DVSA Guide to Tractor and Specialist Vehicle Driving Tests
The Official DVSA Theory Test for Approved Driving Instructors (DVD-ROM)

Acknowledgement
Photographs on pages 29, 30 and 45 reproduced by kind permission of Honda.

We're turning over a new leaf.

RECYCLED
Paper made from
recycled material
FSC® C002151

Find us online

> GOV.UK – Simpler, clearer, faster

GOV.UK is the best place to find government services and information for

- car drivers
- motorcyclists
- driving licences
- driving and riding tests
- towing a caravan or trailer
- medical rules
- driving and riding for a living
- online services.

Visit **www.gov.uk** and try it out.

You can also find contact details for DVSA and other motoring agencies like DVLA at **www.gov.uk**

You'll notice that links to **GOV.UK**, the UK's new central government site, don't always take you to a specific page. This is because this new kind of site constantly adapts to what people really search for and so such static links would quickly go out of date. Try it out. Simply search what you need from your preferred search site or from **www.gov.uk** and you should find what you're looking for. You can give feedback to the Government Digital Service from the website.

Driver & Vehicle Standards Agency

The Driver and Vehicle Standards Agency (DVSA) is an executive agency of the Department for Transport.

We improve road safety in Great Britain by setting standards for driving and motorcycling, and making sure drivers, vehicle operators and MOT garages understand and follow roadworthiness standards. We also provide a range of licensing, testing, education and enforcement services.

www.gov.uk/dvsa

The Driver and Vehicle Agency (DVA) is an executive agency within the Department of the Environment for Northern Ireland.

Its primary aim is to promote and improve road safety through the advancement of driving standards and implementation of the government's policies for improving the mechanical standards of vehicles.

nidirect.gov.uk/motoring

⊙ Contents

Section nineteen | Riding abroad

⊕ A message from the Chief Driving Examiner

Motorcycling can be an enjoyable and exhilarating experience, as well as an economic means of transport. However, the volume of traffic on the roads and the trend towards faster, more powerful motorcycles make it essential, more than ever before, for riders to be ready to deal with the unexpected. After all, it's in your interest to make safety your responsibility.

Whether you're an experienced motorcyclist or a new rider, you'll realise that riding not only requires skill in handling your machine, but also the ability to 'read' the road. Good observation and anticipation are essential to safe riding.

This book is a step-by-step guide to motorcycling, covering all aspects: from choosing your machine and the correct protective clothing to defensive riding and the importance of proper training. It's an essential reference book for all motorcyclists, however experienced – and for instructors too. Read it carefully and put into practice the advice it gives.

Above all, make sure that your aim is safe riding for life.

Lesley Young
Chief Driving Examiner

Section one

⊙ The rider

This section covers

- Your attitude
- Health
- New riders
- Returning riders
- Older riders
- Disabled riders

⊕ Your attitude

Riding a motorcycle can be great fun and is enjoyed by people of all ages. However, riding on the road means accepting responsibility for your actions and showing care and consideration for all other road users. No matter how fast, expensive or efficient your motorcycle is, it's you, the rider, who determines whether it's a safe means of transport.

Being a good rider doesn't mean being a perfect rider – in fact, it's very doubtful whether a perfect rider exists. A good rider is someone who knows that they can always get better and is willing to make the effort.

With experience your practical skills will improve, but that alone won't make you a good rider. To achieve that goal, you'll need to look at the way you approach your riding. Your machine, clothing, the road, the weather and the traffic all have an important influence on your safety, but **you** determine the type of rider you become.

When you ride on the road, other people's safety depends on your responsible behaviour.

You need to develop the ability to

- concentrate and not allow yourself to be distracted

- scan the road ahead and all around you, learning to anticipate any risky situations

- be patient with other road users

- understand your own state of mind and health, and how they may affect your riding

- have an awareness of your own abilities.

Be considerate in queuing traffic. You should avoid obstructing junctions, so that the way is clear for turning traffic.

Together, these qualities make up what's generally known as the rider's attitude. It's your attitude, together with personal characteristics such as mood, emotional state, and levels of fatigue and stress, that will affect how you behave on the road.

There's a lot of satisfaction to be gained from showing not only your skill and ability but also courtesy and consideration to those around you.

> **REMEMBER**, nearly all motorcycle road traffic incidents are influenced, to some extent, by the actions of the rider. Riding responsibly and within your own capabilities will help to make you a safer rider.

Responsibility

As a responsible rider, you must always be concerned for the safety of

- yourself

- your passenger

- other road users.

Yourself

Be responsible by recognising your own limitations. See the information on health later in this section for more advice.

Your passenger

Be aware of any particular needs your passenger may have; for example, if they're nervous or are new to riding as a pillion passenger. You must make sure you have the skills, knowledge and ability to carry a pillion passenger safely.

Other road users

Be tolerant; remember that everyone is entitled to use the road. This may mean making allowances for other road users from time to time – particularly the most vulnerable road users, such as

- children and older people
- people with disabilities
- cyclists
- people in charge of animals.

> **REMEMBER**, the responsibility for safe riding rests with you.

Concentration

To be able to ride safely in today's traffic conditions, you must concentrate fully at all times. If you're driving a car, a lapse in concentration may only dent your pride (and your car). Motorcycles aren't so forgiving.

Avoid riding if you're

- feeling tired or unwell
- distracted in any way
- upset or annoyed
- under a lot of mental or emotional pressure.

Concentration is the key to anticipation and is helped by having

- good vision
- good hearing
- good health
- self-discipline.

> **FACTS** A contributing factor in around 42% of collisions attended by a police officer between 2009 and 2012 was that the driver/rider failed to look properly.

If you have any on-board technology, such as a satellite navigation (sat-nav) system, don't let it distract you from riding. Keep any visual or manual interaction with the system to an absolute minimum. You should find an appropriate, safe and legal place to stop before making any adjustments.

Before you set out

- Turn your phone off, put it in silent mode or put it out of reach.
- If you're using a sat-nav, set your destination and make sure the device is positioned correctly.

While on the move, don't

- use your phone
- look at your sat-nav for more than a brief moment
- listen to loud music, as this can mask other sounds
- let yourself be distracted by your pillion/sidecar passenger.

In addition don't

- stick non-essential stickers on the screen of your motorcycle as they may restrict your view.

> **REMEMBER**, your concentration can also be seriously affected by riding when cold and/or wet. Always wear the correct warm and weatherproof clothing if there's any possibility you'll be riding in poor weather conditions.

Mobile phones

Riding requires all of your attention, all of the time. Using any type of phone or communication system can distract your attention from the road. It's safer not to do so while riding. If you need to make a call, stop in a safe place first.

Anticipation

Anticipation means planning well ahead and being prepared to take early action. With experience, it should become an instinctive part of your riding.

You need to continually question the actions of other road users. If you plan ahead and try to anticipate the actions of others, you can

- avoid the need for a sudden reaction
- maintain a comfortable safety margin
- prevent some hazards from developing
- save fuel by anticipating situations early. Braking late and heavily, then accelerating as the situation improves, increases fuel consumption.

Take early action in response to those hazards that do develop.

Find a safe place to stop before making a call. Let your incoming calls go to voicemail while you're riding, and stop before checking your messages.

You also need to consider

- the road – how sharp is the next bend? What's around the next corner? Can you stop within your range of vision? Road signs and road markings are there to help you plan ahead
- the conditions – you'll be exposed to the weather and affected by the road conditions. Slippery surfaces are especially dangerous for motorcyclists.

Anticipation and good planning are essential to the development of defensive riding techniques.

Patience

If you're upset by the bad behaviour of another road user, try not to react. If necessary, slow down to calm yourself, even if you feel like making a more aggressive response. Consider stopping to take a break. While your brain is processing strong emotions, such as anger, your attention can be taken away from your riding. As a result, your powers of concentration, anticipation and observation are likely to be greatly reduced. This will make a road traffic incident more likely.

We all make mistakes from time to time, so be prepared to make allowances for someone else's mistakes.

REMEMBER, your actions can affect the behaviour of other road users. Setting a good example can have a positive effect on their riding/driving.

Do

- keep calm
- show restraint
- use sound judgement.

Don't

- ride in an aggressive or competitive way
- use aggressive language or gestures
- try to teach another road user a lesson, even if they've caused you inconvenience.

> **REMEMBER**, not every vehicle showing L plates (or D plates in Wales) is fitted with dual controls, and the person accompanying the driver might not be a professional instructor. (!)

Learner drivers and riders

Be patient if the vehicle ahead of you is being driven or ridden by a learner. They may not be as skilful at anticipating and responding to events as a more experienced road user.

Don't

- ride up close behind a learner, as this is intimidating and could cause them to panic

- show your impatience (for example, by revving your engine) if the learner is slow to move off

- cut in sharply after overtaking.

Expect a learner to make mistakes. Allow for their mistakes and don't give them a hard time. Learners may not take the action you expect, and it may take them longer to do things. Don't forget we were all learners once.

The volume of traffic on today's roads inevitably leads to congestion and delays. Showing patience and restraint will help keep you safe and sets a good example.

Drivers who have recently passed their test may display a green P plate or other warning sign to alert others that they're new drivers. Be patient and make allowances for their lack of experience.

Older drivers

Although they have more experience, older drivers may have slower reactions than younger drivers. Make allowances for this.

Planning your journey

- Make sure your motorcycle is roadworthy. For example, check your lights, indicators, oil level, and tyre condition and pressure.

- Plan refuelling stops.

- Check the weather to see whether it's likely to affect your journey.

- If it's a long journey, plan enough time for breaks and refreshment.

- If you have a sat-nav, program it before you start out. Select the route you prefer and think about traffic congestion and times of day, as this can help you to avoid delays and save fuel.

- Don't rely on your sat-nav alone, as it may have out-of-date or incomplete information at any given time. Use road and street maps as well, or check your route on the internet.

- Give yourself plenty of time for your journey. Hurrying leads to mistakes, and mistakes can lead to incidents.

You can keep up to date with the latest traffic and travel news by visiting these websites.

In England
trafficengland.com

In Scotland
trafficscotland.org

In Wales
traffic-wales.com

For information about local roads, visit your council's website.

You can also plan your journey by listening to travel news on local and national radio.

The weather

The weather is an important factor when you're riding. If it's really bad, it might be best to postpone your trip or use public transport. Always try to avoid riding in thick fog or icy conditions. It's a much greater strain, and the risk of a road traffic incident is far higher.

Many riders run into difficulties in very bad weather. Follow the weather forecasts and general advice to drivers/riders through local and national media.

Riding close to home

Many road traffic incidents happen close to home, on regular or routine journeys. If you ride to work every day, don't leave yourself the bare minimum of time to get there.

Don't let familiarity with your home area and surroundings lead you to start taking risks simply because you feel you know every detail.

Remember that strangers won't have the benefit of local knowledge, so they might drive more cautiously than you feel they should.

 Health

Your eyesight

All drivers and riders must be able to read, in good daylight, a post-2001 number plate from 20 metres. Glasses or corrective lenses may be worn if necessary. If you have any doubts about your vision, you should consult an optician.

For more information on riders' and drivers' eyesight requirements, visit **www.gov.uk**

Fitness to ride

You must

- be medically fit to ride

- understand that some medicines shouldn't be taken if you intend to ride. Check with your doctor that it's safe to ride if you're taking any prescription medicine

- notify the Driver and Vehicle Licensing Agency (DVLA) in Swansea, or the Driver and Vehicle Agency (DVA) in Northern Ireland, if your health is likely to affect your ability to ride either now or, because of a worsening condition, in the future.

Don't ride if you're feeling tired or unwell. Even a cold can make it unsafe for you to ride. If you find you're losing concentration or not feeling well, keep your speed to a safe minimum and give yourself more time to react. Stop and take a break as soon as you can.

It's also important to be physically fit to ride. You must have full control of your motorcycle at all times. Remember that, for example

- a twisted ankle can affect your use of the foot controls

- a stiff neck can make it difficult to look behind you when taking necessary observation or checking blind spots.

Alcohol

Alcohol will seriously impair your judgement and your ability to ride safely. You must be aware that

- riding with alcohol in your blood is potentially very dangerous. There are severe penalties if you ride or attempt to ride while over the legal limit

- if you drink in the evening, you might still be over the legal limit and unfit to ride the following morning.

Alcohol is removed from the blood at the rate of about one unit an hour, but this varies from person to person. If you know how many units you've had, you may be able to work out roughly how many hours it will take for your body to be alcohol-free. To be on the safe side, you should start counting from when you had your last drink. If you have any doubts, don't ride or drive. Remember that the only safe limit, ever, is zero.

To be absolutely sure there's no alcohol left in your body the morning after drinking, you can check yourself with a home breath-testing kit.

You **MUST NOT** ride a motorcycle or moped if your breath alcohol level is higher than the legally permitted level – see **www.gov.uk**

REMEMBER, if you drink, don't ride – and if you ride, don't drink.

The alcohol limits for riders in Scotland are different from those for riders in England, Wales and Northern Ireland. See the following website for more information.

www.gov.uk/drink-drive-limit

Drugs

It's illegal to ride a motorcycle or moped in England and Wales if

- you're unfit to do so because you've taken legal or illegal drugs
- you have more than the specified levels of certain illegal drugs in your blood (even if they haven't affected your riding)
- you have more than the specified levels of certain prescription medicines in your blood and you haven't been prescribed them.

You should note that the levels of illegal drugs specified in the legislation are very low, and are only there to allow for cases of accidental exposure. The government has a zero-tolerance approach to people who drive or ride after taking illegal drugs.

Legal drugs include prescription medicines and over-the-counter medicines. If you're taking these medicines and you aren't sure whether you should ride, talk to your doctor, pharmacist or healthcare professional.

If the police think you might have taken drugs, they can stop you and make you do a 'field impairment assessment'. This is a series of tests; for example, asking you to walk in a straight line. They can also use a roadside drug kit to screen for cannabis and cocaine.

If the police think you're unfit to ride because you've taken drugs, you'll be arrested and you'll have to take a blood or urine test at a police station. If this test shows that you've taken drugs, you could be charged with a crime.

> **REMEMBER**, although the new drug-driving law doesn't cover Scotland or Northern Ireland, you can still be arrested if you're unfit to drive.

> For more information about the drug-driving laws, visit this web page.
>
> **www.gov.uk/drug-driving-law**
>
> Watch this video from Think! to learn more about the effects of drugs on road safety.
>
> **http://think.direct.gov.uk/video-drug-driving-lights.html**

Fatigue

Fatigue can mean that you feel tired, sleepy or lacking in energy. Symptoms can include

- slower reflexes
- poor decision making
- headaches
- lack of concentration
- muscle weakness
- irritability.

Riding while you're tired increases your risk of being involved in a collision, so don't ride for too long without taking a break. It's recommended that you take a break of at least 15 minutes after every two hours of riding. This is especially important at night.

Don't begin a journey if you feel tired – make sure you get a good night's sleep before starting a long journey.

Try to avoid riding between 2.00 am and 7.00 am, because this is when the 'body clock' is in a daily dip.

If you begin to feel sleepy, stop in a safe place before you get to the stage of 'fighting sleep'. Sleep can come upon you more quickly than you would imagine. Also, when you're very tired, you can experience microsleeps, which means that you could lose consciousness for up to 30 seconds.

If it isn't possible to stop immediately, stop as soon as it's safe and legal to do so. On a motorway, pull in at the nearest service area or leave the motorway. The only time you may stop on the hard shoulder of the motorway is in an emergency, so you **MUST NOT** stop there to rest.

The most effective ways to counter sleepiness are caffeine and a short nap. The combination of a caffeinated drink (for example, caffeinated coffee), followed by a short nap of up to 15 minutes, is particularly effective. Caffeine takes 20–30 minutes to be absorbed and act on the brain, which will give you the opportunity for a nap. However, this shouldn't be used as a long-term solution to your sleepiness.

Other factors

Being cold and wet

You can get very cold and wet when riding a motorcycle, especially if you aren't wearing appropriate clothing. Hands and feet are particularly susceptible. Being cold and wet will reduce your ability to concentrate and will slow your reactions.

Worries

If something upsets or worries you, think twice before starting a journey. If you can't concentrate on your riding, consider using some other means of transport.

After a shock

A shock or bereavement can badly upset your concentration. As when you're angry, if your brain is dealing with something intense – like anxiety or grief – your attention can be taken away from your riding. In this situation, avoid riding altogether.

⊕ New riders

New riders are vulnerable because they lack experience on the roads. They can be involved in incidents early in their motorcycling careers. Young riders may be especially vulnerable.

Incidents involving new riders are usually caused by

- lack of experience and judgement
- competitive behaviour, racing and lack of consideration for others
- being overconfident in their own ability
- the natural spirit of youth and a tendency to push boundaries
- showing off to friends.

If you're a new rider, avoid

- riding too fast; speed reduces the time you have to react, and increases the force of the impact if you're involved in a collision
- riding without consideration and care
- showing off; if you want to impress your friends, show them how safe a rider you are

- being 'wound up'; keep calm
- an aggressive attitude and behaviour
- riding beyond your capabilities; always leave yourself a safety margin
- being distracted.

Above all, be responsible and show courtesy and consideration to other road users.

False perceptions

Many young motorcyclists wrongly believe that fast reactions and the ability to handle their machine will make them a good and safe rider. They fail to recognise that handling skills alone won't prevent road traffic incidents.

Having the right attitude and a sound knowledge of defensive riding techniques is essential.

The enhanced rider scheme

The Driver and Vehicle Standards Agency (DVSA), in partnership with training experts, has developed a package of training known as the enhanced rider scheme.

The scheme is intended to benefit everyone with a full motorcycle licence, irrespective of experience, including those who have just passed their test. The training is bespoke and designed to address individual needs. Riders who undertake the training may qualify for discounts from those insurance companies that have signed up to the scheme.

To find out more about the enhanced rider scheme, or to look for a post-test motorcycle trainer in your area, visit **www.gov.uk**

The Think! Road Safety 'Never too good' campaign encourages motorcyclists to undertake further training.

http://think.direct.gov.uk/video-motorcycles-never-too-good.html

⊙ Returning riders

If you return to motorcycling after an absence of several years, you'll probably find that a lot has changed. This will include

- road and traffic conditions
- motorcycle technology
- your skills.

You may have picked up habits from driving a car that have a detrimental effect when riding a motorcycle. It's important to understand how braking and cornering techniques on two wheels differ from those used in a car.

If you hold a full motorcycle licence from years ago, it's recommended that you seek refresher training before taking to the road on a modern motorcycle. Many approved training bodies (ATBs) provide this training, and it's a good way to refresh your skills in a safe and enjoyable manner.

> You can find a local ATB by visiting
>
> **www.gov.uk/compulsory-basic-training-cbt-courses**
>
> and entering your post code.

⊙ Older riders

Although they're experienced, older riders can also be vulnerable, but for different reasons. The natural and gradual deterioration in physical fitness and ability that comes with age can affect judgement and concentration.

If you're an older rider, be responsible and

- have your eyesight, including your night vision, checked regularly. It's common for eyesight to deteriorate with age. If you find you need glasses for riding, you **MUST** wear them whenever you ride
- avoid riding at night if you find the glare from headlights dazzles you
- be aware that you may find riding more tiring as you get older
- be honest with yourself about your riding. If you believe that you're no longer safe on the road, it may be time to stop riding.

You might choose to limit your riding by not using your motorcycle

- to travel long distances
- at rush hour
- in bad weather.

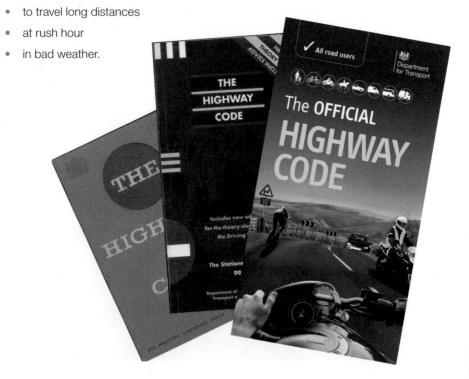

> **REMEMBER,** recognise your own limitations. Don't take risks.

➡ Disabled riders

Disabled riders can be more susceptible to fatigue and should always consider this important factor when planning a journey.

If you're a disabled rider

- Don't overstretch yourself on a long journey. Trying to keep up with people who don't suffer fatigue in the way you do can put you and other road users at unnecessary risk.

- Know your limits and stay within them. Disabled riders shouldn't think they have anything to prove to other people.

Some riders find that adaptations to their motorcycle can greatly reduce fatigue. You can find more information about adaptations in section 5.

> **REMEMBER,** fatigue can only be detrimental to your riding skills and your level of concentration.

Section two

⊙ The rider and the law

This section covers

- Compulsory basic training
- Motorcycle riders
- Moped riders
- Foreign licence holders
- Disqualified riders
- New Drivers Act
- Vehicle documents
- Insurance

⊕ Compulsory basic training

All learner motorcycle and moped riders (with certain exceptions – see below) must complete a course of compulsory basic training (CBT) before riding on the road. CBT can only be given by approved training bodies (ATBs) that have

- trainers who have been assessed by the Driver and Vehicle Standards Agency (DVSA)
- sites approved by DVSA for off-road training.

CBT allows you to safely learn

- motorcycling theory
- the skills that will make you safe on the road
- the correct attitude.

Many people find CBT is an enjoyable activity and an opportunity to meet like-minded motorcyclists.

You don't have to take CBT if you

- passed a full moped test after 1 December 1990
- live and ride on specified offshore islands
- already hold a full category A, A1 or A2 licence.

CBT may be taken on a direct access motorcycle (see 'Obtaining a motorcycle licence', later in this section). If you have this type of motorcycle, you may find that some of the initial parts of CBT are covered on a standard learner machine.

CBT completion certificate (DL196)

When you've completed CBT, you'll be given a DL196. Keep this safe. You must have a DL196 before you can take the practical motorcycle test.

The DL196 will record whether CBT was completed on a two-wheeled machine or on one with more than two wheels (see 'Disabled riders', below) and will validate your provisional entitlement accordingly.

Certificate life

CBT certificates have a two-year life. If you don't pass a practical riding test within this two-year period, you must take CBT again.

A certificate validating full moped entitlement on a full car licence will remain valid for mopeds for the life of the licence.

Disabled riders

CBT may be completed on

- a solo moped or motorcycle

or, if you're disabled, on

- a motorcycle/sidecar combination
- a motor tricycle (trike)
- a moped that has more than two wheels.

Note: a full car driving licence predating 19 January 2013 includes a full trike entitlement. This will remain valid for trikes for the life of the licence.

 **Motorcycle riders**

Motorcycle licence requirements

To ride a motorcycle on the road, you must be at least 17 years old and hold a driving licence that allows you to ride motorcycles (category A, A1 or A2). That licence can be any of the following

- a provisional driving licence – this provides provisional car, motorcycle and moped entitlement
- a full motorcycle licence
- a full car licence – this provides provisional motorcycle entitlement
- a full moped licence – this provides provisional motorcycle entitlement.

> **Where can I get a driving-licence application form?**
>
> Forms are available from
>
> * post offices
> * vehicle registration offices
> * the Driver and Vehicle Licensing Agency (DVLA)
> * **www.gov.uk**

Provisional motorcycle entitlement

After completing CBT (see the start of this section), learners may ride a solo motorcycle

* up to 125 cc
* with a power output of no more than 11 kW
* displaying red L plates (or D plates in Wales) to the front and rear of the motorcycle.

Full motorcycle licence

Since 19 January 2013, there have been three categories of motorcycle licence: A, A1 and A2. The table below explains what you can ride and at what age.

Category	Description	Minimum age
A1	A motorcycle with a cylinder capacity not exceeding 125 cc, of a power not exceeding 11 kW (14.6 bhp) and with a power-to-weight ratio not exceeding 0.1 kW per kg	17
	A motor tricycle of a power not exceeding 15 kW	17
A2	A motorcycle of a power not exceeding 35 kW (46.6 bhp), with a power-to-weight ratio not exceeding 0.2 kW per kg and not being derived from a vehicle of more than double its power	19
A	Any motorcycle	24*
	A motor tricycle of a power exceeding 15 kW	24**

* Age 21 if you have two years' experience on an A2 motorcycle and you pass a further practical test

** You can ride/drive a motor tricycle at age 21 with a full car driving licence

Am I required to take a theory test?
All candidates for a practical motorcycle test must first pass a theory test, unless they're taking the progressive access route and are upgrading from A1 to A2 or A2 to A.

What are the rules concerning test motorcycles?
Motorcycles with an engine size smaller than 120 cc aren't acceptable for the practical motorcycle test.

Only disabled people can use a trike or a motorcycle-and-sidecar combination for the test. Any licence they obtain will be restricted to such combinations.

If you pass your test on a motorcycle with automatic or semi-automatic transmission, this will be recorded on your licence. Your full licence entitlement will be restricted to motorcycles with this type of transmission.

Progressive access
Riders who wish to progress from category A1 to A2 or from A2 to A must pass a practical test to obtain each licence category. This test will only be available when the licence for the lower category has been held for at least two years.

Old licence category	New licence category	Minimum test vehicles EU requirements from 19 January 2013	Min age limit	Access requirements
P	AM mopeds	Two-wheeled machine with a cubic capacity of no more than 50 cc and a maximum design speed not exceeding 45 km/h (28 mph).	16	CBT, theory and practical tests
A1	A1	Motorcycle without a sidecar, with a cubic capacity of at least 120 cc, no more than 125 cc, and a power output not exceeding 11 kW (14.6 bhp), capable of a speed of at least 90 km/h (55 mph).	17	CBT, theory and practical tests
No previous category	A2	Motorcycle without a sidecar, with a cubic capacity of at least 395 cc, an engine power between 20 kW (26.8 bhp) and 35 kW (46.6 bhp), and a power-to-weight ratio not exceeding 0.2 kW/kg. If restricted, not derived from a vehicle more than double its power.	19	**(Progressive access)** Held A1 licence for a minimum of 2 years – take a practical test **(Direct access)** Hold a valid CBT and theory test certificate and take a practical test.
A	A	Motorcycle without a sidecar, with a cubic capacity of at least 595 cc and an engine power of at least 40 kW (53.6 bhp).	21 24	**(Progressive access)** Held A2 licence for a minimum of 2 years – take a practical test **(Direct access)** Hold a valid CBT and theory test certificate and take a practical test.

* Restricted motorcycles – Any switchable or variable restriction device must be installed by a reliable source and certified with documentary evidence from a main dealer, an official importer or a recognised specialist in restricting vehicles. It must be clearly evident to the examiner which power mode it is set to. An ECU or power controller that has a clearly visible, switchable power setting would be acceptable for test. Interchangeable carburettor heads/exhaust manifold restrictor or a hidden ECU would not be acceptable for multi-category testing. Any machine which is being used for multiple categories (A2 and A) must be easily recognisable as to which category it is presented for. Evidence of restriction should be in the form of a certificate or on headed paper from an official source such as a main dealer, official importer or recognised specialist in restricting vehicles and must show the vehicle registration number. You'll only need to show the certificate once unless you're using the vehicle at more than one test centre. You're advised to store a copy on the motorcycle; for example, under the saddle.

Other rider information

New riders from 19 Jan 2013 onwards – Moped entitlement will show on licence as 'AM, Q'. See access requirements. If you pass your car test first, you will have the moped entitlement but will have to pass CBT to ride one on the road.

Existing riders with entitlement gained before 19 Jan 2013 – If you already have moped entitlement, you will keep it (engine size up to 50 cc and max speed up to 50 km/h). On new/replacement licences issued to you, this will show as categories AM, P and Q. To retain your existing entitlement, P extends the AM category to include two- or three-wheeled mopeds with a higher speed of up to 50 km/h. If you already have motorcycle entitlement it won't change under the new rules.

This licence category covers small motorcycles up to 11 kW and 125 cc, and motor tricycles with a power output not more than 15 kW.

A three-wheeled moped or motorcycle is only suitable for test if the distance measured between the centre of the area of contact with the road surface of the two wheels is less than 460 millimetres (46 cm).

This licence category covers medium motorcycles up to 35 kW.

DVSA will accept

- evidence from manufacturers or official importers that a specific model of motorcycle meets these requirements

- an individual machine that has been restricted to comply for test as long as you show certified proof of restriction to the examiner. A dyno test certificate is not acceptable.

When wishing to move up to bigger motorcycles, remember that you will be classed as a learner on the larger machine and **MUST NOT** ride it on motorways until you have passed the appropriate test in that category.

This licence category covers motorcycles of unlimited size and power, with or without sidecar, and motor tricycles with a power output of more than 15 kW.

DVSA will accept evidence from manufacturers or official importers that a specific model of motorcycle meets these requirements and will publish this information where it applies to a number of machines of a specific type. Dyno certificates are not acceptable.

When wishing to move up to bigger motorcycles, remember that you will be classed as a learner on the larger machine and **MUST NOT** ride it on motorways until you have passed the appropriate test in that category.

B1 tricycle entitlement gained before 19 Jan 2013 – If you held category B1 entitlement (tricycles and quads) before 19 January 2013, when you renew or replace your licence it will be shown as categories B1 and A (limited to tricycles). You will not be allowed to ride any motorcycle that you previously were not entitled to ride.

A valid theory test certificate is always required before taking the first practical motorcycle test and, unless taking the progressive access route, a valid theory test certificate is required before taking any subsequent practical tests on a bigger motorcycle.

Tricycles – You'll need to follow the same rules if you want to ride a tricycle that falls within these categories. PLEASE NOTE that tests for mopeds with three or four wheels (see exception above), A1 tricycles, A tricycles and motorcycles with sidecars will only be offered to disabled riders.

Categories A and A2 – Additional machines can be added to the list of those known to comply if there's enough evidence that they meet the new rules; this should be either a certificate or on headed paper from an official source such as the manufacturer, a main dealer or an official importer. The candidate is responsible for making sure the machine meets the new rules; if their machine doesn't comply, their test may be cancelled and they may lose their test fee. Different arrangements apply to candidates with a physical disability.

For information and further updates, visit **www.gov.uk**

Obtaining a full motorcycle licence

Category A1

A full category A1 licence allows you to ride light motorcycles with an engine not exceeding 125 cc and a power output of up to 11 kW (14.6 bhp). To obtain a category A1 licence, you must

- successfully complete a CBT course
- pass the motorcycle theory test
- pass the practical motorcycle test on a motorcycle
  - with a cubic capacity of between 120 cc and 125 cc
  - with a power output of up to 11 kW (14.6 bhp)
  - capable of a speed of at least 90 km/h (55 mph).

Category A2

A full category A2 licence allows you to ride machines with a power output of up to 35 kW (46.6 bhp). To obtain a category A2 licence, you must

- be at least 19 years old
- successfully complete a CBT course
- pass the motorcycle theory test
- pass the practical motorcycle test on a motorcycle
  - with a cubic capacity of at least 395 cc
  - with a power output of between 20 kW and 35 kW (between 26.8 bhp and 46.6 bhp)
  - with a power-to-weight ratio not exceeding 0.2 kW/kg
  - that, if restricted, isn't derived from a machine more than double its original power.

Category A2 under progressive access
Alternatively, you can take a category A2 practical test under progressive access. If you already have an A1 licence that you've held for at least two years, you don't need to

- take another theory test
- hold a current CBT certificate.

Under direct or progressive access, you can practise on any size of motorcycle that exceeds the UK learner specification, provided that

- you meet the age requirement for the category of machine you want to ride
- you're accompanied at all times by a qualified approved trainer, who is on another motorcycle and in radio contact with you
- fluorescent or reflective safety clothing is worn during supervision
- red L plates (or D plates in Wales) are fitted and provisional licence restrictions are followed.

Category A

A full category A licence gives you entitlement to ride all motorcycles. You can obtain a category A licence either under progressive access or, at age 24 or over, under the direct access scheme.

Category A under progressive access

You can take a category A practical test at age 21 if you already have an A2 licence that you've held for at least two years. You don't need to

- take another theory test
- hold a current CBT certificate.

A valid theory-test pass certificate will be required if you wish to upgrade at age 24 and you haven't held your A2 licence for 2 years.

Category A under direct access

This is for riders aged 24 and over. To obtain a category A licence, you must

* successfully complete a CBT course
* pass the motorcycle theory test
* pass the practical motorcycle test on a motorcycle with a power output of at least 40 kW (53.6 bhp).

Under direct or progressive access, you can practise on any size of motorcycle that exceeds the UK learner specification, provided that

* you're accompanied at all times by a qualified approved trainer, who is on another motorcycle and in radio contact with you
* fluorescent or reflective safety clothing is worn during supervision
* red L plates (or D plates in Wales) are fitted and provisional licence restrictions are followed.

Full licence entitlement

With a full motorcycle licence, you may

* ride without L plates (or D plates in Wales)
* carry a pillion passenger
* use motorways.

> Visit this website to see a flow chart of the different ways you can get a full motorcycle licence.
>
> **www.gov.uk/government/publications/the-routes-to-your-motorcycle-licence**

Helmets

All motorcycle riders must

* wear a safety helmet at all times when riding, unless they're a member of the Sikh religion and wear a turban
* ensure any helmet, visor or goggles used conform to BSI or EU standards.

⊕ Moped riders

What is a moped?

A moped is a motorcycle that

- has an engine capacity of no more than 50 cc
- has a restricted maximum speed (see below)
- weighs no more than 250 kg.

If the moped was registered before 1 August 1977, its maximum design speed mustn't exceed 50 km/h (about 32 mph). Mopeds built after June 2003 are restricted to 45 km/h (28 mph).

Moped licence requirements

To ride a moped on the road, you must be at least 16 years old and have a licence that entitles you to ride mopeds. At the age of 16, you can apply for a provisional moped licence (category AM).

If you're 17 or over, you can also ride a moped with

- a full car driving licence (see below)

- a full motorcycle licence
- a provisional driving licence – this provides provisional car, motorcycle and moped entitlement.

Provisional moped entitlement

After completing CBT (see the start of this section), you may ride a solo moped displaying red L plates (or D plates in Wales) to the front and rear. You **MUST NOT**

- carry a pillion passenger
- ride on motorways.

Full car licence holders

Holders of a full car driving licence obtained by passing their driving test before 1 February 2001 have unconditional full moped entitlement.

Holders of a full car driving licence obtained by passing their driving test on or after 1 February 2001, who don't already hold a full moped or motorcycle licence, **MUST** have a valid CBT completion certificate (DL196) to validate their full moped entitlement.

If a valid DL196 is already held when the car test is passed, the full moped entitlement will be validated immediately.

A DL196 validating full moped entitlement on a full car licence will remain valid for mopeds for the life of the licence. It's therefore important that the DL196 is kept safe.

> **REMEMBER**, the DL196 that validates your full moped entitlement also validates your provisional motorcycle entitlement for 2 years.

Full licence entitlement

With a full moped licence, you may

- ride mopeds without L plates
- carry a pillion passenger.

> **REMEMBER**, a moped **MUST NOT** be ridden on motorways, even if you hold a full licence.

> Visit this website for more information about riding a moped.
>
> **www.gov.uk/ride-motorcycle-moped/overview**

Helmets

All moped riders must

- wear a safety helmet at all times when riding, unless they're a member of the Sikh religion and wear a turban
- ensure any helmet, visor or goggles used conform to BSI or EU standards.

⊕ Foreign licence holders

Visitors and new residents with a full, valid EC/EEA motorcycle licence may use that licence to ride a motorcycle in Great Britain until they're 70 years old, or for three years after becoming resident in Great Britain, whichever is longer. If your EC/EEA licence was obtained by exchanging a non-EC/EEA licence, you may ride on your licence in Great Britain for no more than 12 months.

Those with licences from outside the EC/EEA may ride a motorcycle in Great Britain for up to 12 months from the date they last entered or became resident in this country. After this period, they must obtain a full British licence.

If you come from certain designated countries (see **www.gov.uk** for more details), you may exchange your full driving licence for a British one within five years of becoming a resident. If you come from any other country, you can obtain a full British licence by applying for a British provisional licence, completing CBT and passing the theory and practical tests.

You must make sure that

- your licence is valid
- you have entitlement for the size of motorcycle you intend to ride
- you're aged 17 or over.

You must apply for a British licence before riding if

- you don't have the correct motorcycle entitlement
- you aren't entitled to ride in Great Britain on your foreign licence, as detailed above.

If you want to take a motorcycle theory test or practical test in Great Britain, you must hold either a British provisional licence or an EU licence.

To book a test with an EU licence, you'll need a UK driver number. To obtain this, you should complete DVLA form D9. DVLA will then issue you with a D91, which will confirm your UK driver number.

⊙ Disqualified riders

Tough penalties exist for anyone convicted of dangerous riding or driving.

Courts will impose an extended test on anyone convicted of dangerous driving or riding offences. They can also impose an extended test on anyone convicted of other offences involving obligatory disqualification.

If you've been disqualified for other endorsable offences, the courts can order a normal-length test before you can recover a full licence.

> View your licence information (and check any penalty points or disqualifications you may have) on this website.
>
> **www.gov.uk/view-driving-licence**

Recovering a full licence

A rider subject to a retest can apply for a provisional licence at the end of the disqualification period. The normal rules for provisional licence holders will apply.

You'll have to take the theory test before you can apply for either an extended or normal-length practical test. If you've been disqualified, your DL196 is rendered invalid by the disqualification, so you'll also have to retake CBT.

Whether you take an extended or normal-length on-road test (module 2), you'll first have to pass the off-road test (module 1).

The extended test

The extended motorcycle or moped test involves about 70 minutes of riding. The test routes cover a wide variety of roads, usually including dual carriageways.

A rider has to

- maintain a satisfactory standard of riding throughout the extended test period
- cope with a wide range of road and traffic conditions.

The examiner will apply the same standard of assessment as for an ordinary test. However, the length of the test and the wide variety of road and traffic conditions make the extended test more demanding. Candidates should make sure they're well prepared before applying.

Higher fees
The higher fee for the extended motorcycle test reflects the longer duration of the test.

Visit this web page for more information about the extended test.

www.gov.uk/driving-disqualifications/disqualification-until-test-pass-or-extended-test-pass

---

⊙ New Drivers Act

Special rules apply for the first two years after you pass your first practical test.

Your licence will be revoked if the number of penalty points on your licence reaches six or more as a result of offences you commit before the two years are over. Offences you committed before passing your test will be taken into account.

You must then reapply for a provisional licence. CBT will have to be completed again and all learner restrictions will apply until you pass the theory and practical tests again.

⊙ Vehicle documents

Vehicle registration certificate (V5C)

A vehicle registration certificate (V5C), also known as a logbook, contains information about the vehicle. It shows

* the name and address of the vehicle's registered keeper

- information about the vehicle, including the make, model and engine size
- the date the vehicle was first registered.

> **REMEMBER**, the registered keeper is the person who keeps the vehicle on a public road. This person isn't necessarily the legal owner of the vehicle, and a V5C isn't proof of ownership.

If you buy a new vehicle
Your dealer will see that you receive one of these certificates.

If you buy a second-hand vehicle
Make sure that you're given the document. You shouldn't buy a vehicle without a V5C – and it should be an original, not a photocopy. The original document is a good indication that the vehicle hasn't been stolen.

Updating and replacing your V5C
It's your legal responsibility to keep the details on your V5C up to date. You must tell DVLA when

- you change your address
- you change your name
- you change any of the details of your vehicle (for example, its colour)
- you no longer have the vehicle.

You can update your V5C by filling in the relevant section and sending the whole form to DVLA, which will issue a new V5C free of charge. Informing DVLA ensures your V11 (tax reminder) is sent to the correct address, enabling you to tax your vehicle.

When a vehicle is sold, both the seller and the buyer must complete and sign the V5C and the seller must send the relevant part to DVLA.

You can get more information about the V5C on the form itself, or from **www.gov.uk**

If you lose or mislay your V5C, you can request a replacement from DVLA, although a fee may be charged.

You can find out what information DVLA holds about a vehicle by visiting this website.

www.gov.uk/get-vehicle-information-from-dvla

Vehicle tax

You can pay your vehicle tax online at **www.gov.uk**. Alternatively, you can use DVLA's automated phone service on **0300 123 4321** or visit certain post office branches.

The paper tax disc is now a thing of the past. You still have to pay your vehicle tax, but you no longer receive a paper disc to display on your motorcycle.

When you buy a vehicle, the tax is no longer transferred with it; you need to pay the tax yourself before you can use the vehicle. You can do this online, by telephone or at the post office, using the New Keeper Supplement (V5C/2) part of the V5C.

DVLA will send you a renewal reminder through the post when your existing vehicle tax is about to run out.

When you sell a vehicle, you should tell DVLA. They'll automatically send you a refund for any full calendar months left on your vehicle tax.

The registered keeper of a vehicle also needs to tell DVLA when the vehicle is off the road, or has been sold, transferred, scrapped or exported; otherwise they remain liable for taxing it. Once DVLA has been notified about a sale or transfer, or that the vehicle is off-road, it will issue an acknowledgement, which should be kept as proof that the vehicle record has been changed.

If you don't relicense your vehicle
Keepers who fail to relicense their vehicle (or make a SORN – see below) incur an automatic penalty. DVLA carries out a computer check each month to identify untaxed vehicles. It's no longer necessary for the vehicle to be seen on a public road before a penalty is issued, but on-road enforcement will continue.

Vehicle tax rates

Rates are set according to the following classes of motorcycle

- not over 150 cc
- 151–400 cc
- 401–600 cc
- over 600 cc.

Statutory Off-Road Notification (SORN)

If you don't intend to use or keep the vehicle on a public road, you can make a SORN and then you won't have to pay vehicle tax. Once you've made a SORN, it will remain valid until the vehicle is taxed, sold or scrapped.

You can make a SORN by

- applying online at **www.gov.uk**
- contacting DVLA on **0300 123 4321** or minicom **0300 790 6201**
- filling in a SORN declaration form V890 and sending it to DVLA. These forms are available from licence-issuing post office branches or can be downloaded from **www.gov.uk**
- filling in the relevant section of your renewal reminder form V11 and taking it to a licence-issuing post office branch
- using form V14 Application for a refund of vehicle tax, if you're also applying for a refund and the vehicle is to remain in your possession.

Older motorcycles

Older motorcycles may be classed as 'historic' and as such are exempt from vehicle tax. If you have an older motorcycle, check with DVLA to find out if it qualifies.

Vehicle test certificate

If your motorcycle is more than three years old, it **MUST** have a current MOT test certificate (unless it's exempt – see below). You won't be able to renew your vehicle tax without it.

The purpose of the MOT test is to ensure that your vehicle's key safety and environmental systems and components meet the required minimum legal standards. The test must be carried out every year by a vehicle testing station appointed by DVSA.

You can have your vehicle tested as much as one month before the current certificate runs out. The expiry date of the new certificate will be one year after the expiry date of the old one.

> **REMEMBER**, an MOT test certificate isn't a guarantee that the vehicle will remain roadworthy and comply with the minimum standards of the certificate. Neither does it imply that the engine and transmission systems are in good condition.

Failure

If your vehicle fails the MOT test and you want to continue to use it, you must make arrangements to have the necessary repairs carried out without delay. The vehicle must pass a retest before it's used on the road, except when

- riding it away from the testing station after failing the test (provided that the current MOT certificate is still valid)
- riding to or from a garage carrying out the repairs
- riding to an MOT test appointment booked in advance.

Even in these circumstances, you can still be prosecuted if your vehicle isn't roadworthy under the various regulations governing its construction and use. In addition, check that your insurance cover remains valid.

Appeals

If you consider the vehicle has been incorrectly failed, details giving information on the right to appeal may be obtained at vehicle testing stations or at **www.gov.uk**

Fees

Ask any vehicle testing station about their current test and retest fees.

Exempt vehicles

Motor vehicles manufactured before 1 January 1960 are exempt from the requirement to have an MOT, although they can be submitted for a test voluntarily.

Owners are still legally required to ensure that these vehicles are safe and in a proper condition to be on the road.

⊕ Insurance

The registered keeper of a vehicle **MUST** make sure the vehicle has motor insurance unless it's kept off the road and a SORN has been made (see 'Vehicle tax', earlier in this section). As part of Continuous Insurance Enforcement (CIE), the registered keeper will be notified when their vehicle appears to be uninsured. If they don't act on the letter and insure the vehicle, they'll risk

- a fixed-penalty fine of £100
- a court prosecution and a fine of up to £1000
- having the vehicle clamped, seized and destroyed.

There are different rules for vehicle insurance in Northern Ireland – see **nidirect.gov.uk**

It's the driver's responsibility to make sure that they're insured to drive the vehicle they're using. Uninsured drivers can now be detected by the police and roadside automatic number-plate recognition (ANPR) cameras, which are linked to the motor insurance database. The penalties for uninsured drivers include

- an unlimited fine
- 6–8 penalty points on their licence
- having the vehicle seized by the police, taken away and destroyed.

Motor insurance can be arranged online or in person with an insurance company, broker or other insurance provider.

Types of insurance

Third party

This is the legal minimum and generally the cheapest insurance cover. 'Third party' means anyone you might injure or whose property you might damage. You aren't covered for damage to the motorcycle you're riding or injury to yourself.

Third party, fire and theft

This is the same as third party, except that it also covers you in the event of your motorcycle being stolen or damaged by fire.

Comprehensive

This is the best type of insurance, but the most expensive. Apart from covering injury to other persons and damage to their property, it also covers damage to your motorcycle.

Pillion passenger insurance

Most policies include cover for a pillion passenger. This is much the same as for car passengers. Before carrying a pillion passenger, check that your policy includes this cover.

Cost of insurance

This varies with

- your age – the younger you are, the more it will cost
- the make of your motorcycle
- the power and capacity of the engine
- where you live.

Engine-size groups for insurance purposes can vary from one insurer to another. This is another reason to shop around when looking for insurance cover.

What's insured

This also varies from company to company. Read the small print and ask your insurer or broker. Shop around and buy the best policy you can afford.

You'll often have to pay an agreed amount towards any claim. This is called the 'excess'.

Certificate of insurance

This is a simple document that certifies

- who's insured to use the vehicle
- the vehicle covered
- the type of insurance cover
- the period of cover
- the main conditions.

Sometimes a broker will give you a temporary certificate or 'cover note' while you're waiting for the certificate. A cover note normally lasts for one month.

Keep your insurance certificate safe. You'll need to produce it

- if the police ask you to
- if you're involved in an incident.

The policy document

This contains the full details of the contract between you and the insurance company, and how to claim. Insurance companies also supply a summary of the main terms and conditions. If there's anything you don't understand, ask your broker or the insurance company to explain.

Section three

→ Choosing a motorcycle

This section covers

- Buying a motorcycle
- Types of motorcycle

⊕ Buying a motorcycle

Motorcycles come in many different types and sizes. Some of the main types of motorcycle and their features are described over the next few pages. You need to think carefully before deciding which one to buy.

Apart from buying the machine, you'll have to consider insurance, running costs and clothing. You'll also need to consider the location of the nearest dealer.

You can get further information from manufacturers' brochures, the internet, magazines and newspapers. Talking to other riders can give you another point of view. However, the final choice is always yours.

Riders with disabilities

Disabled people who may require adaptations to their motorcycle or its controls should seek advice on the suitability of the machine they intend to purchase. Independent advice is available from the National Association for Bikers with a Disability (NABD) via **nabd.org.uk** or by telephone on **0844 415 4849**.

Budgeting

Costs you'll have to think about include

- purchase price – this may determine whether you buy new or second-hand
- insurance – some models cost a lot more to insure than others
- running costs – fuel consumption and the cost of new tyres and other spare parts need to be considered
- clothing – if you're new to motorcycling, the cost of a helmet, gloves, jacket, boots, etc can be a major consideration.

Type of motorcycle

When choosing a machine, you'll need to ask yourself about

- your licence – are you entitled to ride motorcycles of any engine size? Check your licence category. For more details, visit **www.gov.uk**

- suitability – what do you want from your motorcycle? A small commuter machine is going to struggle with long-distance motorway riding
- comfort – are you comfortable on the machine? Can you reach the controls easily? Can your feet reach the ground?
- weight – some motorcycles are very heavy. This can present problems when parking or manoeuvring.

Motorcycle dealers

The motorcycle dealership in your area could influence your decision. Being able to have your machine serviced locally could be important to you. A dealer can also

- offer finance packages
- offer part-exchange deals
- offer special insurance rates
- arrange training courses
- let you try out a motorcycle before you make a final decision (subject to your licence entitlement)
- give you expert advice.

⊙ Types of motorcycle

Motorcycles are categorised primarily by engine size and power output. For a full explanation of the different licence categories and the sizes of motorcycle that you can ride under these categories, see section 2.

Beyond that, motorcycles come in various styles and with different features. Some of these are described on the following pages.

Automatic motorcycles

Automatic or semi-automatic motorcycles are easier to ride than machines with full manual transmission. They're ideal for short trips and for use in heavy town traffic.

You can take your motorcycle test on an automatic motorcycle. However, if you pass, your full licence entitlement will be restricted to such machines.

Custom motorcycles

Sometimes called 'cruisers', these motorcycles are recognisable by their unique styling. They

- are available in a wide range of engine sizes, including 125 cc
- usually have a low seat height
- have a 'laid back' riding position.

Sports motorcycles

Sports motorcycles have racing styling. They come in a variety of engine sizes and can be

- expensive to buy and run
- capable of very high speed.

When you ride this type of machine for the first time, take care. You may find yourself going faster than you intended.

Touring motorcycles

Touring motorcycles are designed for comfortable long-distance riding. They feature

- a relaxed riding position
- luggage-carrying capacity
- some form of fairing for weather protection
- a large engine.

Off-road motorcycles (trail bikes)

Trail bikes are designed to be used both on and off the road. This type of motorcycle

- comes in a wide range of engine sizes
- has extra ground clearance, which increases the seat height
- is often fitted with dual-purpose tyres
- is built to cope with riding over rough ground.

Section four
⊙ **Clothing and protection**

This section covers

- Visors and goggles
- Safety helmets
- Protective clothing
- Gloves
- Boots
- Visibility aids
- Motorcycle fairings
- Other protection

⊕ Visors and goggles

A visor or goggles are vital to protect your eyes from wind, rain, insects and road dirt. All visors and goggles must

- comply with one of these British Standards
  - BS 4110 Grade X, or
  - BS 4110 Grade XA, or
  - BS 4110 Grade YA, or
  - BS 4110 Grade ZA
- display a BSI kitemark

or

- comply with a European standard that offers a level of safety and protection at least equivalent to these British Standards and carry a mark equivalent to the BSI kitemark (ECE 22-05).

Goggles may comply with the EU Directive on Personal Protective Equipment and carry the 'CE' mark.

Glasses and tinted eyewear

If you normally wear glasses or contact lenses, you **MUST** wear them when you ride. Don't wear tinted glasses, visors or goggles if you're riding in the dark or in conditions of poor visibility.

Cleaning your visor or goggles

It's important that you keep your visor or goggles clean. You must have a clear view of the road ahead at all times. To clean your goggles or visor, wash them in warm soapy water or follow the manufacturer's specific instructions. Don't use solvents or petrol.

In cold and wet weather, your visor or goggles might fog up on the inside. You can either use a special anti-fog spray or fit an anti-mist visor insert to your helmet to help prevent this. If your visor or goggles fog up while you're riding, choose somewhere safe to stop and wipe them with a clean cloth. Carry a cloth with you for this purpose.

Damaged or scratched goggles and visors

Scratches on your visor or goggles can distort your view and cause dazzle from the lights of oncoming vehicles at night. They can also cause glare, especially from low winter sun.

If your visor or goggles are heavily scratched, buy new ones.

⊕ Safety helmets

By law, you must wear a safety helmet when riding a motorcycle on the road. (Members of the Sikh religion who wear a turban are exempt.)

All helmets sold in the UK must

- comply with British Standard BS 6658: 1985 and carry the BSI kitemark, or

- comply with UNECE Regulation 22.05 (the helmet will be marked with a UN 'E' mark; the first two digits of the approval number will be '05'), or

- comply with any standard accepted by a member of the European Economic Area (EEA) that offers a level of safety and protection equivalent to BS 6658: 1985 and carry a mark equivalent to the BSI kitemark.

The Safety Helmet Assessment and Rating Program (SHARP) offers you a single, easy-to-understand rating for helmets.

> To find out more about motorcycle helmets and the law, visit this website.
>
> **http://sharp.direct.gov.uk**

Types of safety helmet

Motorcycle helmets are either full face or open face.

Full-face helmets
This type of helmet

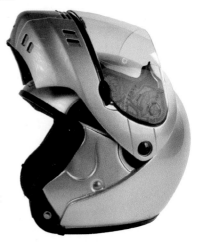

- covers the head fully and has a hinged visor
- protects the face in a road traffic incident
- offers more weather protection than an open-face helmet.

Open-face helmets
This type of helmet is preferred by riders who feel closed in by full-face helmets. It can be worn with either a visor or goggles, but it doesn't protect the chin in an incident.

Flip-up helmets
These are open-face helmets with a hinged front that closes to resemble a full-face helmet. The visor can be opened or closed independently of the hinged front. Make sure that you lock the chin guard down before riding.

Helmet fit

When you buy a new helmet, it should be a good, snug fit. The padding will soon bed down and this could make the helmet loose. A loose helmet isn't only uncomfortable; it could also come off in a collision.

Helmet fastening

Helmets normally use one of three different fastening methods: double D-ring, quick release, and bar and buckle.

Some helmet straps also have a Velcro® tab to secure the strap, so that it doesn't flap in the wind. This Velcro tab isn't to be used to fasten the helmet. It's both unsafe and illegal to ride with a helmet that's unfastened or incorrectly fastened.

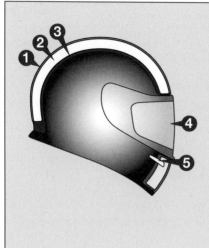

1 Outer shell Designed to disperse the force of an impact in the event of an incident.

2 Crumple zone This expanded polystyrene layer is designed to absorb the remaining force of the impact.

3 Comfort layer Comprises different types of foam to provide a comfortable fit.

4 Visor Made from strong polycarbonate, this protects the rider's face.

5 Ventilation A source of fresh air and helps to remove exhaled humidity.

Helmet materials

The outer shell of motorcycle safety helmets is made from one of three basic materials: polycarbonate, glass fibre and Kevlar®.

Polycarbonate
- lighter than glass fibre
- mustn't be painted or have stickers affixed
- mustn't be cleaned with solvents
- tends to be cheaper than other types and doesn't last as long.

Glass fibre
- heavier than polycarbonate
- lasts longer than polycarbonate
- easy to clean.

Kevlar
- extremely tough
- used as a composite with glass fibre, or carbon and glass fibre
- combines great strength with light weight
- tends to be expensive.

Damage to helmets

If your helmet receives any serious impact, buy a new one. A damaged helmet could be unreliable in a road traffic incident.

Damage won't always be visible to the naked eye. For this reason, never use a second-hand helmet. Repairs to damaged helmets aren't recommended.

⊕ Protective clothing

Clothing is available that will keep you warm and dry in all but the worst conditions. If you allow yourself to become cold and wet when riding, you'll lose concentration.

Protective clothing for motorcyclists is designed to protect you from the cold and wet, and, just as importantly, from some kinds of injury. Always wear your protective clothing, whatever the weather. If you fall from your motorcycle, this clothing is the only barrier between you and the hard road surface.

Clothing that a manufacturer either claims or implies to have protective properties (other than protection from the weather) must be marked with the 'CE' mark.

Protective clothing for motorcyclists may be made from man-made materials or leather.

Man-made materials

Nylon is the most popular material giving protection from the weather. It's available in many different forms and comes under many different brand names. Other materials, such as waxed cotton, are also available.

More expensive garments have reinforcing and padding at the shoulders and elbows. This provides some protection in the event of a road traffic incident.

Generally, man-made outer clothing is designed to fit over your normal clothes. It can come as a jacket and trousers or a one-piece suit, and is available lined or unlined.

When you're buying outer clothing, make sure that you have enough room for extra layers of warm clothing underneath and that your movement isn't restricted.

Leathers

Motorcyclists have traditionally worn leathers. These offer a high degree of protection from abrasion if you fall off your machine. They come in several different types.

One-piece suits

Leather motorcycle suits aren't designed to fit over your normal clothes. They do, however, offer the motorcyclist certain advantages, including reduced wind resistance and a high degree of windproofing.

They also have some disadvantages; for example, they're expensive to buy.

Leathers are usually only showerproof (you'll have to use a waterproof oversuit in wet weather) and they aren't warm. Due to the close fit, you can't wear extra layers underneath in cold weather and you may experience some restriction of movement.

Two-piece zip-together suits

These comprise a separate jacket and trousers, which zip together. This style has some advantages:

- you can buy the jacket or trousers separately. This lets you spread the cost to suit your budget. It also lets you buy different sizes to suit you
- zipping the jacket and trousers together helps to stop draughts around your waist
- the jacket or trousers can be worn separately.

Separate jacket and trousers

This option

- is often the least expensive
- gives you a wide choice of styles, colours, sizes and prices.

When you're choosing leathers, look for additional protection for shoulders, elbows and knees.

Visit your motorcycle dealer or motorcycle clothing supplier. Try on various types of clothing for fit and comfort. As a general rule, buy the best you can afford.

⊙ Gloves

Good gloves are essential when you ride a motorcycle. Never be tempted to ride without gloves. If you fall off, you could seriously injure your hands.

Your gloves should

- protect your hands from cold and wet weather
- protect your hands if you fall off
- allow you to operate the controls easily.

Materials

Leather is one of the most suitable materials for motorcycle gloves. Cheaper materials don't provide the same level of protection. On its own, leather is tough, supple and resistant to water, but when combined with modern materials and construction methods it can be used to make waterproof gloves.

For protection from prolonged rain, you may need to wear gloves made from waterproof man-made materials.

 Boots

It's important to wear appropriate protective footwear when you ride a motorcycle. If you wear sandals or trainers, your feet will have little protection.

Approved motorcycle boots

- protect your feet from cold and wet weather
- offer some protection if you're involved in a collision
- protect your feet and shins from knocks and bumps.

Types of boots

Two types of material are used for motorcycle boots: leather and man-made materials.

Leather is strong, flexible and weather resistant. This makes it the most suitable material for motorcycle boots. Leather boots give the best protection in the event of a road traffic incident. They're available either unlined or lined.

Boots made from leather combined with modern materials and construction techniques can resist water, even in the wettest conditions. However, leather alone isn't totally waterproof and you might need to wear overboots in very wet weather.

Boots made from man-made material can offer better weather protection and may be cheaper than leather. You can buy them lined or unlined.

Whichever type of boot you decide to buy, make sure that

- they're comfortable
- you can operate the foot controls easily.

Try as many different boots as you can, and always buy the best you can afford.

> If your boots have laces, make sure the laces are fastened correctly, so they don't get caught in the chain or any controls.

⮕ Visibility aids

Many road traffic incidents involving motorcyclists occur because other road users don't see them. Using some form of visibility aid will help others to see you.

In daylight

Wearing fluorescent orange or yellow clothing will improve your chances of being seen in daylight. This can be

- a fluorescent jacket
- a fluorescent tabard or waistcoat
- a fluorescent 'Sam Browne' belt.

You need to be visible from the side, as well as from the front and back.

Other methods you could use to help other road users to see you in daylight include

* wearing a white or brightly coloured helmet and brightly coloured clothing
* having your headlights on dipped beam.

In the dark

To improve your visibility in the dark, you need to wear reflective material. This can take the form of belts, patches or strips. These work by reflecting light from the headlights of other vehicles, making you much more visible from a long distance away.

Reflective strips on your gloves will help other road users to see your arm signals.

⊕ Motorcycle fairings

Motorcycle fairings come in three main types

* half fairings
* full fairings
* sports fairings.

Half fairings

These mainly protect your head and upper body, and are most common on middleweight machines.

Full fairings

These are usually found on touring motorcycles. They provide weather protection to the hands, legs and feet, and also make higher-speed riding more comfortable by giving protection from the wind.

A typical touring fairing

A typical sports fairing

Sports fairings

These give some weather protection, but they're mainly intended to reduce wind resistance.

⊙ Other protection

Noise

Motorcyclists are exposed to a lot of noise, both from their motorcycle's engine and from air turbulence around their helmet.

This constant noise can cause

- fatigue
- hearing damage.

Wearing ear plugs helps to reduce the fatigue caused by noise and can also prevent hearing damage.

The noise caused by wind turbulence can also be reduced by

- using a fairing or windscreen. This needs to be tall enough to channel the wind over the rider's head. A screen that's too low may cause increased noise by directing the air flow at the rider's helmet
- choosing a helmet that's designed to reduce this noise.

Cold

When you're riding in cold weather, low temperatures are further reduced by wind chill. Good motorcycle clothing should keep you warm and dry, but your hands and feet are exposed and vulnerable to the chilling effect. You can very quickly lose all feeling in your fingers and toes. This can affect

- your ability to control your motorcycle
- your concentration.

To overcome the cold affecting your hands, you can try wearing thin inner gloves, while an extra pair of socks can help to keep your feet warm.

If you start to lose feeling in your hands or feet, you should stop and warm up before continuing with your journey.

If you regularly ride in cold weather, electrically heated equipment is available to help overcome the effects of low temperatures. This includes heated

- handlebar grips
- gloves
- boot insoles
- inner jackets.

Before buying electrically heated equipment, check that your motorcycle's electrical systems can cope with the additional demands this equipment creates.

A fairing or screen that keeps the air flow off you can also help to prevent the chilling effect of the wind.

Protection for disabled riders

People with disabilities involving reduced sensory function, such as paralysis from spinal injury or brachial plexus injuries, should be aware that the effects of cold due to bad weather and/or wind chill may be much harder to detect in the affected limbs and extremities. In severe cases, this can lead to frostbite. In some cases, people with paralysis due to spinal injury can also experience a marked increase in the likelihood of muscle spasms if they allow the affected limbs to become too cold.

The effects of cold and wind chill can also be much more acute for people who suffer circulatory problems, such as those related to diabetes or hypotension, and can cause increasing discomfort and/or stiffness in joints that have been damaged or are affected by arthritis.

Disabled motorcyclists frequently use

- electrically heated glove liners
- socks and/or under-clothing.

This clothing is designed to counteract the amplified effects of wind chill on damaged limbs or arthritic joints.

Heated under-clothing for motorcyclists is usually powered by a small pack of rechargeable batteries that clip onto the user's belt.

In cases where amputation or the deformity of a limb due to illness or injury makes standard heated clothing unsuitable, items can be tailor-made to suit the needs of the individual.

Back protector

Back or spine protectors are designed to protect your spine in the event of a collision or a fall from your motorcycle.

Back protectors can be an integral part of your jacket or a separate garment that's worn under your jacket. A separate spine protector can be either

- full length, covering most of the length of your spine, or
- a lumbar protector, designed to support your lower back.

Separate spine protectors are firmly strapped to your body to prevent them from moving around, and are made from rigid, semi-rigid and flexible materials.

Section five
→ Motorcycle controls

This section covers

- Instrument panel
- Handlebar controls
- Foot controls
- Anti-lock braking systems
- Traction control and linked braking systems

⊙ Instrument panel

Before you ride any motorcycle, make sure you're familiar with the layout of all the controls and switches. While control layouts are generally similar, there may be differences in their feel and method of operation.

For detailed information and guidance on the specific instruments fitted to a motorcycle, see the vehicle handbook.

Visual aids

The main visual aids on the instrument panel are

- speedometer
- rev counter
- milometer (odometer)
- fuel gauge
- temperature gauge.

Speedometer

This tells you how fast the motorcycle is travelling, in miles per hour (mph) and kilometres per hour (km/h). It's usually a dial with a needle showing the speed, but it may alternatively be a digital display.

Rev counter

This shows the engine speed in revolutions (revs) per minute. If you allow the revs to reach the red-coloured numbers, damage to the engine may occur.

Many motorcycles have a safety device called a rev limiter. This prevents the engine from revving beyond its safe limits. If you're riding a motorcycle and the rev limiter activates, you'll feel a sudden drop in power. This can happen if you forget to change up to the next gear. Closing the throttle or changing up a gear will cause the revs to fall and the limiter will immediately deactivate.

Milometer (odometer)

Usually housed in the speedometer, this shows the total number of miles or kilometres travelled by your motorcycle. A separate trip meter can be used to record the length of a journey or to help calculate fuel consumption.

Fuel gauge

Most modern motorcycles are fitted with a fuel gauge. This makes it easier to know when you need to refuel.

If your motorcycle isn't fitted with a fuel gauge, you need to take care to avoid running out of petrol. As a rough guide, you can peer into the tank to see the level of fuel remaining. Alternatively, you can keep a note of how many miles you've covered since you refuelled, or wait until the fuel runs onto the reserve supply. (This usually involves a change to the setting of the fuel tap.)

Running onto reserve is best avoided, as your motorcycle will run unevenly or possibly cut out before you can set the fuel tap to the reserve position. This can be dangerous; for example, if your main fuel supply is used up as you're emerging at a busy junction.

Your motorcycle may have a fuel gauge and a low-fuel warning light. If the low-fuel warning light shows, don't delay in seeking a filling station.

Temperature gauges are fitted to motorcycles with liquid-cooled engines and not to those fitted with air-cooled engines.

Temperature gauge

Fitted to motorcycles with liquid-cooled engines, this gauge shows the coolant temperature and so can warn you if the engine is overheating. If you see that the gauge is climbing towards the red zone, it's best to stop and find out whether there's a problem with the cooling system. The most common fault is a loss of coolant, caused by a leak. Repairing the fault is likely to be a lot easier and cheaper than repairing any damage caused by allowing the engine to overheat.

If the engine overheats, this can lead to an expensive repair and your motorcycle may be off the road for some time.

Warning lights

These lights help you to

- ride safely
- protect the engine and other equipment against damage
- see the function selected.

Many different types of light may be fitted. Red-coloured warning lights indicate a fault that affects safety and needs immediate attention.

Ignition light
This comes on when you switch on the ignition. It should go out when the engine is running. If it doesn't, this indicates a problem with the electrical system.

Oil pressure light
This warns you of low oil pressure. If it comes on when the engine is running, you may have a serious problem. Stop the engine immediately and investigate the cause.

Engine management light
Modern engines are fitted with an engine management system that monitors the fuel/air/exhaust mix and also the ignition system. If the engine management light doesn't go out when the engine is started, or comes on when the engine is running, there's a fault. A garage with diagnostic equipment should be able to identify the reason why the warning light is on and advise you of any repair work needed.

Neutral light
This glows when the gear selector is in the neutral position.

Main-beam light
This indicates that your headlights are on main beam. It reminds you to dip your headlights when necessary.

Indicator repeater lights
These lights tell you that your indicators are flashing. Check the repeater lights to confirm that you've cancelled a signal.

Rear fog light warning light
This alerts you that your high-intensity rear fog light is switched on. When visibility improves and you can see more than 100 metres, you should turn the fog light off to avoid dazzling following drivers.

Hazard warning lights
When your hazard warning lights are activated, all four direction indicators will flash simultaneously and both indicator repeater lights will flash together.

Hazard warning lights should be used to warn other road users, either when you're causing an obstruction (such as when you've broken down) or when you have to slow down quickly on a motorway or unrestricted dual carriageway because of a hazard ahead. Don't use them to excuse illegal or inconsiderate stopping or parking – there are no excuses for this behaviour.

Anti-lock brakes (ABS) warning light
See 'Anti-lock braking systems', later in this section, for more information about this light.

⊕ Handlebar controls

Headlight flasher

This switch lets you flash your headlights. This has the same meaning as sounding your horn. Flash your headlights if your horn may not be heard – for example, on a motorway.

Horn

Sound the horn to warn other road users if you don't think they've seen you.

You **MUST NOT** sound your horn

- between 11.30 pm and 7.00 am in a built-up area
- when your motorcycle is stationary, unless a moving vehicle poses a danger.

Headlight dip switch

This lets you switch your headlights between main beam and dipped beam.

On main beam, you'll usually see a blue warning light on your instrument panel. At night, switch to dipped beam when meeting or following other vehicles. This will stop your lights from dazzling other drivers.

Indicators

You use the indicators to let other road users know that you intend to change direction. You must make sure that you cancel them after turning.

Clutch

The clutch engages and disengages the engine from the drive to the rear wheel.

On a motorcycle with an automatic gearbox, the operation of the clutch is part of an automated process, so no clutch control is fitted.

On a motorcycle with a manual gearbox, changing gear involves the use of the clutch lever on the handlebar. This lever is also used to assist in 'slow control'.

Use the clutch

- when you select first gear before moving off
- to prevent the engine from stalling when you stop
- to change gears
- when selecting neutral.

To change or select a gear

- Pull the clutch lever fully to the handlebar.
- Select the gear you need.
- Release the clutch lever smoothly to engage the clutch.

REMEMBER, the clutch is always on the left handlebar.

Fully automatic motorcycles

This type of motorcycle has no clutch lever. Often, the rear brake lever is fitted in place of the clutch lever.

Semi-automatic motorcycles

These have no clutch lever. The clutch operates automatically when you use the gear-change pedal.

Some motorcycles may also have a hand-operated style of gear selection.

Clutch control for disabled riders

Some disabled riders choose to use a motorcycle with automatic transmission. However, there are also options for people who wish to maintain manual control. Some manufacturers offer purpose-made twin-lever units, which enable the motorcycle to be converted to a right-hand-operated system. It's also possible to convert the clutch to a left-foot-operated system.

Engine management

On some motorcycles, you can alter the power output of the engine to suit different weather or riding conditions. The engine management control allows you to select settings such as 'Normal riding', 'Sport' or 'Wet weather'.

Choke

A choke is a device that helps when starting a cold engine. It operates by changing the amount of air in the air/fuel mixture that the engine burns.

Most modern motorcycles have fuel injection or an automatic choke, but some older models may have a manual choke.

If your machine has a manual choke and you're starting a cold engine

- Move the choke control to 'on'.
- Start the engine.
- Gradually move the choke control to 'off' as the engine warms up.

Failure to return the choke to 'off' could cause the engine to run faster than normal. This could make it difficult to control the motorcycle, especially when slowing down. In addition, it could cause excessive wear to the engine and increased fuel consumption.

Engine cut-out switch

This switch is designed to stop the engine in an emergency.

When stopping the engine normally, use the ignition switch rather than the cut-out switch, because

- you're less likely to leave your keys in the ignition when leaving your motorcycle
- forgetting that the cut-out switch is in the 'off' position can lead to problems starting the engine again later.

Although you won't normally need to use the cut-out switch, you should check it occasionally to make sure that it operates correctly.

Ignition switch

The ignition switch is usually operated by a key. Turning the key clockwise will switch the engine electrics on. The ignition switch may also be used to engage the steering lock or turn the parking lights on. Not every motorcycle is the same, so check your vehicle handbook for more information.

Electric starter

This is fitted as well as, or in place of, a kick-start lever.

To use an electric starter

- Check that the engine cut-out switch is in the 'on' position.
- Switch the ignition on.
- Make sure that the gear selector is in neutral or that you've pulled the clutch lever in fully.
- Make sure that the side stand is up.
- On a machine with automatic transmission, make sure that the brake is firmly applied.
- Press the starter button.

Light switch

On many newer models, dipped-beam headlights are automatically switched on when the ignition is turned on or the engine is started. With this arrangement, there's no light switch. Parking lights are switched on by moving the ignition key to a 'Park' position.

On motorcycles not fitted with this feature, the light switch is found on the right handlebar and is either a headlight on/off switch or a three-position switch allowing you to select headlights, parking lights or neither.

Front brake lever

This lever applies the brake to the front wheel.

To apply the front brake, progressively squeeze the lever towards you. Use all the fingers on your right hand for maximum control and stopping power. The harder you squeeze, the harder you brake. To release the brake, release the lever.

Motorcycles adapted for disabled riders may feature an adapted front brake lever on the left handlebar. Alternatively, some disabled riders prefer thumb-brake units, which can be mounted on the left or right handlebar and are used to operate the front brake system by pushing forward on a paddle-type lever.

Throttle

The throttle controls the engine's speed by increasing or reducing the amount of fuel delivered to the engine. To speed up the engine, twist the throttle towards you. To slow down the engine, twist the throttle away from you.

Most throttles will spring back to a closed position when released. In this position, the engine should run at 'idle' or 'tick-over' speed.

On motorcycles adapted for disabled riders, the throttle may be fitted to the left handlebar or converted to a thumb-operated throttle similar to the type fitted on quad bikes.

> In cases where cumulative fatigue is a problem, a clip-on throttle adaptation might be helpful.

Mirrors

Mirrors are fitted to both the right and left handlebars, or sometimes to the fairing. They should be adjusted to give you the best view of the road behind. If your elbows obscure the view, try fitting mirrors with longer stems.

Two types of mirror are available

- flat mirrors – these don't distort the image of the road behind. This makes it easier for you to judge the speed and distance of traffic behind you

- convex mirrors – these are slightly curved and give a wider field of vision. However, they make it more difficult to judge the speed and distance of traffic behind you.

⊕ Foot controls

Gear selector

It's important that you select the right gear for the speed at which you're travelling.

Low gears allow the engine to rev freely, giving the rear wheel lots of turning power. Use a low gear when you're moving off, going uphill or accelerating.

High gears allow the motorcycle to travel at a higher speed, but they provide less turning power. They should be used when cruising at a steady speed.

Changing smoothly through the gears is a skill that improves with practice.

Position

The gear selector is usually on the left-hand side of the motorcycle, just in front of the footrest.

Some mopeds and scooters have a twist-grip gear change on the left handlebar.

The gear lever is usually on the left, but on older motorcycles it's often on the right (or even hand-operated on some vintage models).

The green neutral light glows to indicate that the gearbox is in neutral.

Use

Gears are selected by lifting or pushing down the gear lever with your foot. The positions and number of gears vary with the make and model of motorcycle.

As you speed up, you click upwards to go up a gear. As you slow down, you click downwards to go down a gear.

In the neutral position, no gear is engaged. Most motorcycles have a green warning light to show when the gearbox is in neutral.

Rear brake pedal

This pedal applies the brake to the rear wheel.

Position

The rear brake pedal is usually on the right-hand side of the motorcycle, just in front of the footrest. Some automatic motorcycles have a rear brake lever on the left handlebar.

Use

To apply the brake, press the pedal with your foot. To release the brake, release the pedal. Try to avoid resting your foot on the pedal, as this may make the brake lights come on.

Thick-soled riding boots can affect the feel of the rear brake. You could find yourself braking harder than you intended.

On motorcycles adapted for disabled riders, the rear brake pedal may be converted to a hand-operated system using a purpose-made twin-level unit. Alternatively, some manufacturers offer thumb-brake units, which can be mounted on the left or right handlebar and are used to operate the rear brake system by pushing on a paddle-type lever.

Kick-start lever

Most modern motorcycles have electric starters and so kick-starters are less common. However, if your machine has a kick-start lever, you'll usually find it on the right-hand side of the motorcycle, near the footrest.

To use the kick-start lever

- Make sure that the engine cut-out switch is in the 'on' position.
- Switch on the ignition.
- Put the gear selector in neutral and check that the neutral light glows.
- Fold out the kick-start lever. (You may need to fold the footrest out of the way.)
- Tread down sharply on the lever. Repeat until the engine starts.

⊙ Anti-lock braking systems

Anti-lock braking systems (ABS) are designed to prevent wheel lock caused by excessive braking. This can enable the rider to achieve maximum braking when travelling in a straight line. The system can't increase tyre grip or prevent skids where other factors are at work, such as when cornering.

ABS employs wheel-speed sensors to anticipate when a wheel is about to lock under extreme braking. Just before the wheel begins to lock, the system releases the brakes momentarily before automatically reapplying them. This cycle is repeated several times a second to maximise braking performance.

You should refer to the vehicle handbook for details of the manufacturer's recommended method of use.

Knowing that ABS will help you stop safely shouldn't encourage you to ride less carefully. ABS can't overcome the laws of physics; it's still possible for one or both of the tyres to skid because of

- poor road contact
- surface water
- a loose road surface.

ABS warning light

Anti-lock braking systems will have a warning light. Generally, this will light up when you turn on the ignition and may not go out until the motorcycle is travelling at 5–10 mph (8–16 km/h).

Read your vehicle handbook to find out how the system is designed to operate on your motorcycle.

⊕ Traction control and linked braking systems

Traction control systems

Traction control systems (TCS) help to prevent wheelspin when accelerating. This is most likely to occur on slippery surfaces. A sensor detects that the rear wheel is starting to spin and the system adjusts the power driving the rear wheel, so that grip is maintained. A warning light may glow to let you know when TCS is in operation.

TCS may also be activated by riding over a sudden change in road level, such as a hump bridge.

While TCS enables a rider to make maximum use of the tyres' grip during acceleration, it can't prevent loss of grip caused by cornering too fast or failing to take account of road and weather conditions.

Linked braking systems

Some motorcycles have a linked braking system, where use of one brake control activates both the front and rear brakes. However, full braking effectiveness is still achieved by applying both brakes together.

If your motorcycle has a linked braking system, refer to your vehicle handbook for the manufacturer's recommendations on its use.

Section six
➡ Starting to ride

This section covers

- Getting started
- Stands
- Mounting and dismounting
- Starting the engine
- Moving off
- Using the brakes
- Stopping safely
- Emergency braking
- Using the gears
- Signalling
- Moving off at an angle
- Moving off uphill

⊙ Getting started

This section takes you through the basics of motorcycle handling. When you ride in traffic, you must have full control of your motorcycle at all times. This requires a good working knowledge of the various controls and the ability to coordinate your use of the hand and foot controls.

In addition, you need to have

- an understanding of the rules of the road
- respect for the needs of other road users
- sufficient basic knowledge to check that everything is working correctly and the machine is safe before you set out.

Starting to ride isn't just a matter of starting the engine and setting off. You should first of all check your motorcycle to make sure it's safe and ready for the road.

Everyday checks

Make a habit of checking daily that

- there are no oil, petrol or water leaks
- all lights (including indicators) are working; replace any dead bulbs immediately (it's a good idea to carry spare fuses and bulbs)
- the brakes are working; don't ride with faulty brakes. Also check that the wheels and tyres show no sign of damage.

Periodic checks

These checks are both for safety and part of good vehicle maintenance. Check and top up if necessary

- engine oil
- water in the radiator or expansion tank (for liquid-cooled engines)
- brake fluid

- battery – top up with distilled water if necessary (some batteries are maintenance-free and don't need topping up).

You should also check the tyres and make sure they're legal; they must have the correct tread depth and be free of dangerous cuts or other defects. Also check that they're inflated to the right pressure.

> **REMEMBER**, don't ignore a problem or try to cut costs. For example, don't risk using worn or damaged tyres. Safety must never be sacrificed for economy.

Clean your machine regularly. This will help you to identify any leaks, loose items or developing mechanical problems.

How often?
How often you should make the checks depends on how much you ride. Consult your vehicle handbook. If you ride a lot, you may need to carry out these checks every day.

Basic maintenance
Further information about basic motorcycle maintenance can be found in section 15 of this book.

Regular servicing
Have your motorcycle serviced regularly. The vehicle handbook will state the recommended service intervals.

 Stands

When you park a motorcycle, you use a stand to support it. Motorcycles have either a centre stand or a side stand, and many models are fitted with both.

Side stand

The side stand is generally quicker and easier to use than the centre stand. It relies on the motorcycle leaning over onto the stand for stability.

Care must be taken to ensure that

- the surface is firm enough to prevent the side stand from sinking in and the motorcycle falling over
- the surface slope doesn't prevent the motorcycle from leaning on the stand. If the machine is too upright, it will be unstable.

Allow enough room for the stand to rest on the road without catching the kerb.

To put your motorcycle on the side stand

- Apply the front brake and dismount to the left of the motorcycle.
- With the machine upright, push the stand fully down with your foot.
- Let the machine lean towards you until its weight is taken by the stand.
- Turn the handlebars to the left and gently release the front brake.

To take your motorcycle off the side stand

- Position yourself on the left of the motorcycle and apply the front brake.
- Turn the handlebars straight while pushing the motorcycle upright.
- Move the stand to its 'up' position with your foot. Make sure it locks securely.
- Mount the machine from the left.

Most side stands can also be operated while you're sitting astride the motorcycle. To put your motorcycle on the side stand using this method

- Apply the front brake and support the machine with both feet down.
- Push the side stand fully down with your left foot.
- Carefully let the machine lean to the left until its weight is taken on the stand.
- As you dismount to the left, turn the handlebars to the left and gently release the front brake.

To take your motorcycle off the side stand

- Apply the front brake and turn the handlebars slightly to the right while pushing the motorcycle upright.
- Mount the motorcycle from the left and support it upright with both feet down.

- Straighten the handlebars and move the stand to its 'up' position with your left foot. Make sure it locks securely.

Remember that stands are designed only to take the weight of the motorcycle.

If the stand isn't fully up, it could dig into the road when you're cornering and cause a road traffic incident. Some manufacturers fit a safety inhibitor switch to the side stand. Depending on the manufacturer, this prevents

- the engine being started while the side stand is down
- the engine running while the side stand is down
- the engine running if you try to ride off with the side stand down.

If your motorcycle refuses to start or the engine cuts out when you select a gear, it could be that it's fitted with such a safety feature.

As most motorcycle side stands are mounted on the left-hand side, people with a disability that affects their weight-bearing strength in their left leg may find it easier to have a side stand fitted to the right side of the motorcycle. This stand may have to be specially fabricated to allow it to operate without coming into contact with a hot exhaust and/or to allow for the direction of the steering lock on the machine.

Where a disability affects the left leg or ankle to the extent that operating the side stand safely and comfortably isn't possible, a simple linkage can often be fitted to allow the stand to be operated by hand. Alternatively, a small number of engineering companies in the UK can manufacture electrically operated side-stand actuators.

Centre stand

The centre stand gives more stable support than the side stand. It also allows maintenance such as drive-chain adjustment (where fitted) and wheel removal to be carried out.

The centre stand needs to be used on a firm, level surface for maximum stability.

To put your motorcycle on the centre stand

- Position yourself on the left of the motorcycle, holding the left handlebar with your left hand.

- Push the stand down with your right foot (or left foot, if preferred) and hold the frame near the saddle with your right hand (some machines have a special handle).

- Tread down on the stand and pull the machine backwards and upwards.

To take your motorcycle off the centre stand

- Position yourself on the left of the motorcycle.

- Hold the left handlebar with your left hand. Hold the frame near the saddle with your right hand.

- Put your right foot (or left foot, if preferred) firmly on the centre stand.

- Keep the handlebars straight and rock the motorcycle forward. When it comes off the stand, apply the front brake and allow the stand to retract. Lean the motorcycle slightly towards you to keep control.

Disabled riders may find it easier to use a set of free-standing frames known as 'paddock stands'. These frames are hand-operated and slightly lift the motorcycle into a stable position.

>
> **REMEMBER**, if the stand isn't fully up, it could dig into the road when you're cornering and cause an incident.

⊙ Mounting and dismounting

Before mounting or dismounting your motorcycle, look behind to make sure it's safe. Always mount from the left, and dismount to the left, the side away from the traffic.

Before you get on or off, apply the front brake to stop the motorcycle moving.

Practise mounting and dismounting with the motorcycle off its stand.

Balancing and wheeling your motorcycle

After you've practised mounting and dismounting, wheel the machine forward. Leaning the motorcycle slightly towards you makes it easier to balance.

Work the front brake with your right hand to control the speed.

Practise wheeling the machine in circles, both to the left and to the right. Keep practising until you're able to balance and control it fully.

Riding position

When you're seated on a stationary motorcycle, you should be able to

* place both feet on the ground
* use one foot to keep your balance and the other to work the foot controls.

The best posture
Sit in a natural position, as determined by the machine design. You should be able to reach all the controls comfortably.

If you can't operate the hand controls (such as the front brake and clutch levers) comfortably and safely when you're riding, you may be able to adjust them to suit your individual needs. Check your vehicle handbook for more information.

⊙ Starting the engine

The following is a general guide to starting your engine, but you may need to modify it to suit your machine.

To start the engine

- Make sure that the gear selector is in neutral. The neutral light on the instrument panel will glow when the ignition is turned on. If no neutral light is fitted, push your motorcycle forward to check that the rear wheel turns freely.

- Turn the fuel tap (if fitted) to 'on'.

- If the engine is cold, move the choke (if fitted) to 'on'.

- Make sure that the engine cut-out switch is in the 'on' position.

- Turn the ignition key to the 'on' position.

Your motorcycle is now ready to start. The next step depends on whether your machine has an electric starter or a kick-starter.

Electric starter

Press the starter button. As the engine starts, release the button. If necessary, open the throttle a small amount. As the engine warms up, move the choke (if fitted) to 'off'.

Kick-starter

Fold out the kick-start lever. On some machines, you'll have to fold up the footrest before you can use the kick-starter. Place your instep on the lever and tread down sharply. Allow the kick-start lever to return to its upright position. Repeat until the engine starts.

When the engine has started, fold the kick-start lever back to its resting position.

If necessary, open the throttle a small amount. As the engine warms up, move the choke (if fitted) to 'off'.

Stopping the engine

This safe sequence applies to most motorcycles

- Close the throttle fully.
- Make sure that the gear selector is in neutral.
- Turn the ignition key to 'off'. Take out the key in the 'lock' position if you're leaving your machine.
- Turn the fuel tap (if fitted) to 'off'.

⊕ Moving off

To move off safely, you must think about other road users. Can you move off without endangering yourself or anyone else? To answer this question, you need to have a good look around.

> **REMEMBER**, never look down at the front wheel when riding. This can severely upset your balance.

To move off, follow these steps in order

- Sit astride your machine.
- Apply the front brake and then start the engine.
- Squeeze in the clutch lever. Use all your fingers to get full control.
- Select first gear, keeping the clutch lever held in.
- Put your left foot on the ground and shift the weight of the machine to that foot. Put your right foot on the footrest and then apply the rear brake.

Now look around over your right shoulder (unless you're on the right-hand side of the road) and then look ahead. You're looking to make sure that there's no traffic approaching from behind and the way ahead is clear so that it's safe to move off.

Look out for pedestrians and cyclists – they're harder to see than cars. You should signal if it will help any other road user.

It's vital that you look around before moving off, even if you have mirrors fitted. Looking around will allow you to

- judge accurately how far away any traffic may be, and how fast it's travelling
- see if there's anything in the blind area behind and to your right. The blind area is the area that isn't covered by your mirrors (see 'Rear observation', in section 8).

You can now release the front brake and work the throttle.

Clutch control

Release the clutch lever smoothly, until you feel the engine trying to move the machine. This is called the 'biting point'. You must be able to find the biting point easily when releasing the clutch lever. This skill will develop with practice. Open the throttle enough to keep the engine running smoothly.

Gradually release the clutch lever and, at the same time, open the throttle smoothly. As you move off, release the rear brake and bring your left foot up onto the footrest.

Smooth clutch control is essential to good riding. It's also one of the most difficult skills for the novice to acquire.

Steering and turning

Steering a motorcycle at low speeds is a straightforward process, much the same as riding a bicycle. The rider simply turns the handlebars, and therefore the front wheel, in the direction they wish to go. As the machine goes faster, you then need to use a system called 'positive steering' or 'counter-steering' (see section 9).

⊕ Using the brakes

Many motorcycle riders are, quite wrongly, afraid to use the front brake. This is often as a result of what they were taught as cyclists. On a motorcycle

- you must normally use both brakes
- the front brake is the more powerful of the two brakes and the most important when stopping a motorcycle.

To stop most effectively

In good road and weather conditions

- apply the front brake just before you apply the rear brake
- apply greater pressure to the front brake.

Applying greater pressure to the front brake gives the best stopping power in good conditions because

- the combined weight of the machine and rider is thrown forward
- the front tyre is pressed more firmly on the road, giving a better grip.

Coordinating the front and rear brakes correctly is an essential part of riding a motorcycle.

In wet or slippery conditions, you need to apply more equal pressure to the front and rear brakes.

Using only one brake

You'll take much longer to stop by using only one brake. However, at very low speeds (walking pace), using only the rear brake gives smoother control.

When to brake

Always look and plan well ahead to avoid having to brake sharply. A gradual increase in pressure on the brakes is better than late, harsh braking.

Follow these rules

- Brake when your machine is upright and moving in a straight line.
- Brake in good time.
- Adjust the pressure on the brakes according to the road surface and weather conditions.

Where to brake

Where you brake is very important. The best time to brake is when you're travelling upright in a straight line.

Braking on a bend

A good rider will plan well ahead to avoid braking on a bend.

On a bend, the combined weight of the motorcycle and rider is thrown outwards. To balance this, the rider leans inwards.

If you brake on a bend

- the weight will be thrown outwards even more
- the motorcycle and rider may become unstable
- the tyres may lose their grip on the road surface.

If you must brake on a bend

- avoid using the front brake. Rely on the rear brake and engine braking to slow you down. If you must use the front brake, be very gentle. There's a risk of the front tyre losing its grip and sliding sideways
- try to bring your motorcycle upright and brake normally, provided you can do so safely.

⊙ Stopping safely

To stop safely, you need to make sure that you don't endanger any other road users. You should

- use your mirrors and look over your right shoulder, if necessary, to check for traffic behind you
- signal if it will help other road users. People in front may benefit from a signal just as much as people behind.

Stopping

The following sequence will apply to most motorcycles

- Roll off the throttle.
- Apply both brakes smoothly.
- Just before the motorcycle stops, gently ease off the front brake and pull in the clutch lever to avoid stalling the engine.

- As the machine comes to rest, put your left foot on the ground to support the weight.

When the machine has stopped

- Apply the front brake.
- Release the rear brake and support the motorcycle with your right foot.

With the clutch lever still pulled in

- Use your left foot to move the gear selector to neutral.
- Release the clutch lever.
- Place both feet on the ground.

Disengaging the clutch prevents the engine from stalling when the motorcycle stops.

Disengaging the clutch

When stopping from very low speeds, pull in the clutch lever just before or just as you brake.

When stopping from higher speeds, always brake first, then pull in the clutch lever just before you stop.

⊕ Emergency braking

If you plan ahead, you should rarely need to brake violently or stop suddenly. Nevertheless, emergencies do arise, and in these circumstances you must be able to stop safely and quickly.

Maximum braking

- Shut the throttle.
- Use the front brake just before the rear.
- Brake progressively (increase pressure steadily).

- Apply the right amount of braking effort to each wheel. This will depend on the road surface and weather conditions.

- Try to avoid steering and braking at the same time; separate the two inputs by braking first, then releasing the brake before steering, or by steering and then braking.

Braking in an emergency

- Keep your motorcycle upright.

- Apply maximum braking effort without locking the wheels. This is achieved by progressively increasing braking pressure. Don't use the brakes violently, as this may cause you to skid. (See section 8 for more information about skidding.)

- Pull in the clutch just before you stop.

Signalling when you brake

Don't try to give an arm signal when you brake in an emergency, because

- you'll need both hands on the handlebars

- your brake lights will warn traffic behind that you're braking.

Some situations are unpredictable. You'll need to respond quickly and with full control.

➡ Using the gears

To change up or down through the gears, you need to be able to coordinate the clutch, throttle and gear selector.

Changing up

You need to change gear in order to match the engine speed and load to the speed of your motorcycle. This will vary with the vehicle you're riding and whether you're moving on the level, uphill or downhill. As a general rule, however, change up as your road speed increases.

Listening to the engine will help you to determine when to change up. You'll become more familiar with this as you practise, and you'll soon learn to recognise the appropriate level of sound at which to change gear.

To change up

* Simultaneously close the throttle and pull in the clutch lever.
* Select the next higher gear by lifting the gear selector with the toe of your boot. Allow the selector to return to its normal position after each gear change.

How many gears does a motorcycle have?
The number of gears on a motorcycle varies with the make and model. Most modern motorcycles have five or six gears, while some smaller machines have four.

Can I miss out a gear?
The gears on a motorcycle have to be changed sequentially. This means you have to change to the next higher or lower gear in turn. However, it's possible to change to the next gear and, without releasing the clutch, immediately change again until you've selected the gear you require, and then release the clutch.

- Release the clutch lever smoothly and open the throttle at the same time.
- Repeat the sequence for each upward gear change.

Travelling in the highest suitable gear will help you to save fuel and spare your engine.

Changing down

You'll need to change down to a lower gear

- if you've slowed down and the gear you're in doesn't provide enough power at the lower speed
- if you're going uphill in too high a gear and your engine labours or struggles to give enough power
- to increase the effect of engine braking; for example, on a long downhill gradient.

As a general rule

- use the brakes to reduce your speed before changing down to the most suitable gear for the lower speed
- change down to accelerate more quickly or if your speed drops.

To change down

- Simultaneously close the throttle and pull in the clutch lever.
- Select the next lower gear by pushing down the gear selector with the toe of your boot. Allow the selector to return to its normal position after each gear change.
- Release the clutch lever smoothly and open the throttle as necessary.

> **REMEMBER**, riding in a gear that's too high for the road speed makes the engine unresponsive to the throttle.

Finding the right gear

To change gear, you need to anticipate and assess the situation well in advance. Ask yourself whether the gear you're in is correct for that particular situation.

Overtaking

You should consider changing to a lower gear to overtake. A lower gear can give you the power required to accelerate quickly, so that you can pass safely.

Going downhill

When descending a steep hill, a lower gear gives more engine braking and this helps you to keep control.

Judgement

As you become more proficient, you'll be able to judge exactly the gear you need for the speed you intend and the manoeuvre you're planning.

Coasting

Coasting means that, although the vehicle is moving, it isn't being driven by the engine. This occurs either when the clutch lever is held in or the gear selector is in the neutral position.

Coasting for any distance is wrong because

- it reduces your control of the motorcycle
- you might have difficulty engaging a gear if something unexpected happens
- it will almost certainly lead to the vehicle gathering speed when travelling downhill. It means harder braking and it removes the assistance of engine braking in a low gear.

Each time you change gear, you coast a little. This is unavoidable, but it should be kept to a minimum.

Over-run

If the throttle is closed when the vehicle is travelling at speed, the engine may not appear to be 'driving' the vehicle.

This is known as travelling on the over-run and shouldn't be confused with coasting. There's no loss of control, because the vehicle is still in gear and either engine braking or acceleration are available immediately.

Slipping the clutch

This means holding the clutch lever partially in, so that the clutch isn't fully engaged. This allows the engine to spin faster than if it were fully engaged and is often necessary when manoeuvring at slow speeds.

Slipping the clutch to compensate for being in too high a gear at a low speed is bad practice and should be avoided. This can result in excessive wear of the clutch.

⊕ Signalling

You need to give signals to help other road users know what you intend to do.

Road users include

- drivers of following and oncoming vehicles
- cyclists
- pedestrians
- officers directing traffic.

Always signal clearly and in good time. Give only correct signals, as shown in the illustrations.

Arm signals

Arm signals are very effective in daylight, especially when you're wearing bright or fluorescent clothing. However, they aren't a substitute for faulty direction indicators. The law requires that if direction indicators are fitted, they **MUST** work.

Giving an arm signal means that you have reduced steering control, if only briefly, so you should spend some time practising controlling your motorcycle while giving arm signals.

Practise

- with one hand and then with the other
- before you ride on the road.

Give arm signals in good time. Don't try to keep your arm up all the way through a turn. You'll need both hands on the handlebars to make any turn safely.

Arm signals at speed
When travelling at speed on the open road, arm signals can upset your stability. At speed, it's safer to rely on your direction indicators (if fitted).

Arm signals at pedestrian crossings
When slowing down or stopping at a pedestrian crossing, consider giving an arm signal. This tells traffic behind you, approaching traffic and waiting pedestrians that you're slowing down.

REMEMBER, approaching traffic and pedestrians can't see your brake lights.

Direction indicators

The indicator lights on a motorcycle are close together and can be difficult to see. On some smaller machines, they don't show up very well in bright sunlight. You should

- consider giving an arm signal if you think your direction indicators may be difficult to see
- position yourself correctly and in good time for the manoeuvre you intend to perform.

When should I start signalling?
It's important to start signalling before slowing down, braking or changing position. For example, if you wish to turn right but you slow down before giving a signal, a driver behind you may try to overtake.

Do motorcycle indicators automatically cancel after a turn?
A few motorcycles have self-cancelling indicators, but most don't. It's important that the rider makes sure a signal is cancelled after a manoeuvre or there's a real risk of another road user being misled, and this could easily lead to a dangerous situation.

Other signals

Brake lights

These come on when you apply the brakes. On a modern motorcycle, the brake lights are activated by the rear brake pedal and the front brake lever.

The brake lights warn traffic behind you that you're braking. Help other road users by

- braking in good time
- slowing down gradually
- signalling in good time. Give an arm signal if necessary.

Flashing headlights

You should only flash your headlights as an alternative to the horn – to warn others that you're there. Assume that other drivers mean the same. Don't flash your headlights at anyone to invite them to go ahead or turn.

If someone else flashes their headlights, make sure that you understand what they mean and that they're signalling to you. Never assume it's a signal to proceed.

Horn

Sound your horn only if you think someone may not have seen you or to warn other road users of your presence; for example, at a blind bend or junction.

Sounding the horn doesn't give you right of way. Always be prepared to stop.

You **MUST NOT** sound your horn

- between 11.30 pm and 7.00 am in a built-up area
- when your motorcycle is stationary, unless a moving vehicle poses a danger.

Never use your horn as a rebuke or to attract attention.

On high-speed roads, drivers may not be able to hear your horn. In daylight, riding with dipped headlights on can help you to be seen.

Whether using indicators, arm signals, headlights or horn, always think about your signal.

- Is it necessary?
- Is it helpful?

- Is it misleading?

When you signal, do so in good time, clearly and correctly.

Leave other road users in no doubt about your intentions. Giving signals properly is an important part of safe motorcycling.

Timing of signals

Whether you're giving arm signals or using direction indicators

- give your signal early enough to allow other road users to see and act on it
- don't give a signal so early that its meaning could mislead.

Conflicting signals

A signal must have one clear meaning. For example, if you plan to pull up on the left after a junction, you should wait until you've passed the junction before signalling, otherwise other road users may think that you intend to turn left. Avoid giving signals that could have two meanings.

It's important to get into a routine of cancelling your signal after completing a manoeuvre. If you accidentally leave an indicator on, it could mislead other traffic.

Sometimes a hand signal is necessary to reinforce a direction indicator, such as here. The indicator signal alone may be viewed as an intention to move around the obstruction, when actually the intention is to turn right.

⊙ Moving off at an angle

When moving off at an angle – for instance, around a parked car – use the same procedure as for 'Moving off', covered earlier in this section.

Just before you move off, ask yourself

- At what angle should I move out?
- How far will this take me into the road?

Your decision will depend on

- how close you are to the vehicle or object in front
- the width of the vehicle or object
- oncoming traffic.

Check all round for other vehicles, and signal if necessary.

- Give yourself time to steer around the vehicle or object.
- Tight clutch and steering control are needed as you move off. Release the clutch completely as you clear the obstruction.
- If you're moving off around a vehicle, allow room for someone to open a door.
- Be ready to brake – a pedestrian might step out from the other side of the vehicle or object.

Before moving off, it's essential that you look into the areas that aren't visible in your mirrors.

⊕ Moving off uphill

Use the same procedure as for moving off straight ahead, covered earlier in this section.

> **REMEMBER**, allow a safe gap in any traffic, because your motorcycle may be slower to pull away and build up speed.

Be aware that

- your motorcycle will tend to roll back. To avoid this, you must use the throttle, clutch and brakes together
- you may need to use more throttle when moving off uphill than you would when moving off on the level.

The motorcycle will stall if

- you release the rear brake too late
- you release the clutch too quickly
- you don't use enough throttle.

When you've mastered the technique, then practise moving off uphill, without rolling backwards, from behind a parked vehicle.

Section seven
⊙ Traffic signs

This section covers

- The purpose of traffic signs
- Signs giving orders
- Signs giving warning
- Signs giving directions and other information
- Waiting restrictions
- Road markings
- Traffic lights
- Traffic calming
- Level crossings

⊙ The purpose of traffic signs

Signs are an essential part of any traffic system. They tell you about the rules you must obey and warn you about the hazards you may meet on the road ahead.

Signs can be in the form of words or symbols on panels, road markings, beacons, bollards or traffic lights.

To do its job, a sign must give its message clearly and early enough for you to see it, understand it and then act safely on it.

This section deals with the various types of traffic signs and their meaning. For more information, refer to **Know Your Traffic Signs**, which illustrates and explains the vast majority of traffic signs.

Symbols

Symbols are used as much as possible because they're

* more easily recognised and understood
* mainly standardised, particularly throughout Europe.

What are the basic rules when it comes to recognising signs? You'll recognise traffic signs more easily if you understand some basic rules. The shapes and colours of the main groups are:	
	Circular signs These give orders. Blue circles tell you what you **MUST** do, while signs with red rings tell you what you **MUST NOT** do.
	Triangular signs These warn you of something, such as a junction.

	Rectangular signs These inform and give directions.
KEEP CLEAR	**Road markings** These inform, give directions and give orders.
STOP	**Other shapes** A few signs are a different shape altogether as they're very important and need to stand out.

⊕ Signs giving orders

Signs that give orders can be

- mandatory signs: these tell you what you **MUST** do
- prohibitory signs: these tell you what you **MUST NOT** do.

Mandatory signs

These signs are mostly circular, with white symbols and borders on a blue background; for example

- mini-roundabout
- keep left
- turn left.

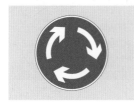  

In addition

- 'stop – children' sign (lollipop) carried by a school crossing patrol. This is circular with black lettering on a yellow background
- 'stop' in white on a red background, often manually controlled at roadworks
- 'stop' and 'give way' signs appear at junctions and are very important for everyone's guidance and safety.

'Stop' signs

These are octagonal, with white lettering on a red background, and are usually found at a junction with a limited zone of vision. The design is deliberately unique so you can tell it apart from other signs. 'Stop' signs are always accompanied by a stop line marked on the road. The line tells you how far forward you should go before stopping to look, assess and decide whether it's safe to proceed.

What you MUST do at 'stop' signs

- Stop (even if you can see the road is clear).
- Wait until you can enter the major road without causing other road users to change speed or direction.

'Give way' signs

These are made up of

- a red triangle pointing downwards
- black lettering on a white background.

They're always accompanied by road markings. However, some junctions only have the 'give way' lines. This is usually where there's relatively little traffic.

'Give way' signs and/or road markings show you that traffic on the road you want to enter has priority.

The double broken lines across the road show you where to stop, if necessary, to take your final look.

What you MUST do at 'give way' signs

- Give way to traffic already on the major road.
- Wait until you can enter the major road without causing any traffic already on the road to change speed or direction.

> **REMEMBER** Look, assess, decide and act.

The 'give way' sign is unique, being the only sign that's a downwards-pointing triangle. This is to ensure that it can be recognised and obeyed, even if you can't see it fully.

Prohibitory signs

These tell you what you **MUST NOT** do.

They're easy to recognise by their circular shape and red border. The message is given by symbols, words or figures, or a combination of these. The exceptions are

- 'no entry' sign (circular with white border and red background)
- 'bus lane' sign.

Speed-limit signs

A red circle with a number on a white background shows the speed limit.

A white disc with a black diagonal line cancels the previous speed limit, but you mustn't exceed the national speed limit for the type of road you're on or the vehicle you're using.

Speed limits

Type of vehicle	Built-up areas* mph (km/h)	Single carriage-ways mph (km/h)	Dual carriage-ways mph (km/h)	Motorways mph (km/h)
Cars and motorcycles (including car-derived vans up to 2 tonnes maximum laden weight)	30 (48)	60 (96)	70 (112)	70 (112)
Cars towing caravans or trailers (including car-derived vans and motorcycles)	30 (48)	50 (80)	60 (96)	60 (96)
Buses, coaches and minibuses (not exceeding 12 metres in overall length)	30 (48)	50 (80)	60 (96)	70 (112)
Goods vehicles (not exceeding 7.5 tonnes maximum laden weight)	30 (48)	50 (80)	60 (96)	70[†] (112)
Goods vehicles (exceeding 7.5 tonnes maximum laden weight) in England and Wales	30 (48)	50 (80)	60 (96)	60 (96)
Goods vehicles (exceeding 7.5 tonnes maximum laden weight) in Scotland	30 (48)	40 (64)	50 (80)	60 (96)

* The 30 mph limit usually applies to all traffic on all roads with street lighting unless signs show otherwise.
† 60 mph (96 km/h) if articulated or towing a trailer.

Be aware that large vehicles may have speed limiters – buses and coaches are restricted to 62 mph and large goods vehicles to 56 mph.

Repeater signs are a smaller form of the original speed-limit sign and are situated at intervals to remind you of the speed limit. In areas where there are regularly spaced street lights, you should assume that the 30 mph (48 km/h) speed limit normally applies, unless there are repeater signs showing a different speed limit.

Test your knowledge of signs by taking the quiz on the Safe Driving for Life website.

safedrivingforlife.info/signsquiz

⊙ Signs giving warning

Usually, this type of sign is a red triangle pointing upwards, with a symbol or words on a white background. These warn you of a hazard you might not otherwise be able to recognise in time; for example, a bend, hill or hump bridge. The sign will make clear what the hazard is. You must decide what to do about it.

Narrowing roads

These signs tell you from which side the road is narrowing (sometimes both sides), and should warn you against overtaking until you've had a chance to assess the hazard.

Children

The warning here is: watch out for children, especially at school start and finish times. Plates may be used with the sign to give extra information, such as 'School', 'Playground' or 'Patrol'. As well as children, look out for school crossing patrols and obey their signals.

Low bridge sign

Even if you're not in a high vehicle, be aware that an oncoming vehicle might have to use the centre of the road to make use of any extra headroom there.

Junctions

These tell you what type of junction is ahead: T-junction, crossroads, roundabout, staggered junction and so on. The priority through the junction is indicated by the broader line.

Sharp change of direction

Chevrons or roadside posts with reflectors may be used

- where the road changes direction sharply enough to create a hazard
- to reinforce a warning sign on a particularly sharp bend.

Other hazards

If there's no special sign for a particular hazard, a general hazard warning sign is used: a red triangle with an exclamation mark on a white background.

There'll be a plate underneath it telling you what the hazard is – for example, a hidden dip.

→ Signs giving directions and other information

These help you find and follow the road you want. They can also direct you to the nearest railway station, car park, or other facility or attraction. The colours of these signs vary with the type of road. For example

- motorways – blue with white letters and border
- primary routes, except motorways – green with white letters and border, route numbers shown in yellow
- other routes – white with black letters and black border.

All these roads may also display tourist signs, which are brown with white letters and border.

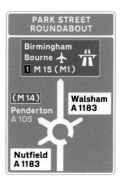

Signs giving directions on primary routes

Advance direction signs
You'll see these before you reach the junction. They enable you to decide which direction to take and to prepare yourself.

Direction signs at the junction
These show you the route to take as you reach the junction.

Route confirmatory signs
Positioned after the junction, these confirm which road you're on. These signs also tell you places and distances on your route. If the route number is in brackets, it means that the road leads to that route.

Information signs
These tell you where to find parking places, telephones, camping sites, etc, or give information about such things as no through roads.

Signs for traffic diversions

In an emergency, when it's necessary to close a section of motorway or other main road to traffic, a temporary sign may advise road users to follow a diversion route. This route guides traffic around the closed section, bringing it back onto the same road further along its length.

To help road users follow the route, black symbols on yellow patches may be permanently displayed on existing direction signs, including motorway signs. An initial sign will alert road users to the closure, then the symbol is shown alongside the route that drivers and riders should follow.

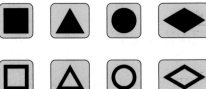

A number of different symbols may be used, as in some places there may be more than one diversion operating. The range of symbols used is shown here.

Drivers and riders should follow signs showing the appropriate symbol. These may be displayed on separate signs, or included on direction signs, giving the number of the road to follow.

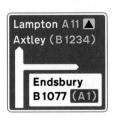

⊕ Waiting restrictions

These are indicated by signs and road markings. Yellow lines along the road parallel to the kerb indicate that restrictions apply.

Small yellow plates may be mounted on walls, posts or lampposts nearby. These give more precise details of the restriction that applies. If there are double yellow lines painted on the road but no plates nearby, there's no waiting at any time.

Controlled parking zones

In controlled parking zones, the times of operation of the zone will be shown on the entry signs. Yellow lines show where waiting is prohibited or restricted, but yellow plates aren't normally provided in these zones.

White bay markings and upright signs indicate where parking is allowed.

Clearways

Some areas and main roads are designated as 'no stopping' zones or clearways. This means no stopping on the main carriageway at any time, not even to pick up or set down passengers.

On urban clearways there's no stopping during the hours of operation except for as long as necessary to set down or pick up passengers.

Red Routes

On many roads in larger cities in the UK, Red Route signs and red road markings have been introduced to replace the yellow-line restrictions. For more information on Red Routes, visit **tfl.gov.uk/redroutes**

⊕ Road markings

Markings on the road give information, orders or warnings. They can be used either with signs on posts or on their own.

Their advantages are

* they can often be seen when other signs are hidden by traffic
* they can give a continuing message as you ride along the road.

As a general rule, the more paint, the more important the message.

Lines across the road

'Give way' lines

Double broken white lines across your half of the road show that traffic on the road you want to enter has priority. The lines show where you should stop, if necessary, to take your final look. These may also be found on a roundabout where traffic on the roundabout is required to give way to those joining.

A single broken line is normally found at the entrance to a roundabout.

This tells you that traffic coming from your immediate right has priority and you **MUST** give way.

Single 'stop' lines

A single continuous line across your half of the road shows where you **MUST** stop

- at junctions with 'stop' signs
- at junctions controlled by traffic lights
- at level crossings and emergency vehicle access points
- at swing bridges or ferries.

Lines along the road

Double white lines

Double white lines have rules for

- overtaking
- parking.

Overtaking

When the line nearest you is continuous, you **MUST NOT** cross or straddle it except when the road is clear and you want to

- enter or leave a side road or entrance on the opposite side of the road
- pass a stationary vehicle
- overtake a pedal cycle, horse or road maintenance vehicle, if they're travelling at 10 mph (16 km/h) or less.

If there isn't room to leave enough space when passing, you should wait for a safe opportunity. Don't try to squeeze past.

If there's a broken white line on your side and a continuous white line on the other side, you may cross both lines to overtake, as long as it's safe to do so.

Make sure you can complete the manoeuvre before reaching a solid line on your side.

Arrows on the road indicate the direction you should pass double white lines or hatch markings. Don't begin to overtake when you see them.

Parking

You **MUST NOT** stop or park on a road marked with double white lines, even if one of the lines is broken, except to pick up or drop off passengers or to load or unload goods.

Hatch markings

There are dangerous areas where it's necessary to separate the streams of traffic completely, such as a sharp bend or hump, or where traffic turning right needs protection. These areas are painted with white chevrons or diagonal stripes and the tarmac areas between them may also be a different colour (for example, red).

In addition, remember

- where the boundary line is solid, don't enter except in an emergency
- where the boundary line is broken, you shouldn't ride on the markings unless you can see that it's safe to do so.

Single broken lines

Watch out for places where the single broken line down the centre of the road gets longer. This means that there's a hazard ahead.

Lane dividers

Short broken white lines are used on wide carriageways to divide them into lanes. You should keep between them unless you're

- changing lanes
- overtaking
- turning right.

Lanes for specific types of vehicle

Bus and cycle lanes are shown by signs and road markings. In some one-way streets these vehicles are permitted to travel against the normal flow of traffic. These are known as contraflow lanes.

Bus lanes

Only vehicles shown on the sign may use the lane during the hours of operation, which are also shown on the sign. Outside those periods all vehicles can use the bus lane. Where no times are shown, the bus lane is in operation for 24 hours a day. Don't use bus lanes when they're in operation unless the sign shows that motorcycles are permitted vehicles.

Cycle lanes

Don't ride or park in a cycle lane marked by a solid white line during the times of operation shown on the signs. If the cycle lane is marked by a broken line, don't ride or park in it unless it's unavoidable. If you park in a cycle lane at any time, you make it very dangerous for any cyclist who's using that lane.

High-occupancy vehicle lanes

Car drivers aren't allowed to use these lanes unless their vehicle contains at least the number of people indicated on the sign. This restriction doesn't apply to motorcyclists: if the sign shows that motorcyclists are allowed to enter the lane, they may do so even when they're riding solo.

Reflective road studs

These may be used with white lines.

- Red studs mark the left-hand side of the road.
- White studs mark the lanes or middle of the road.
- Amber studs mark the right-hand edge of the carriageway on dual carriageways and motorways.
- Green studs mark the edge of the main carriageway at lay-bys and slip roads.

At roadworks, fluorescent green/yellow studs may be used to help identify the lanes in operation.

Box junction markings

Yellow crisscross lines mark a box junction. Their purpose is to keep the junction clear by preventing traffic from stopping in the path of crossing traffic.

You **MUST NOT** enter a box junction unless your exit road is clear. However, you can enter the box when you want to turn right and you're only prevented from doing so by oncoming traffic.

Like all road markings, the yellow painted lines of a box junction can be slippery in the wet.

If there's a vehicle already on the junction waiting to turn right, you're free to enter behind it and wait to turn right – providing that you won't block any oncoming traffic wanting to turn right.

If several vehicles are waiting to turn, it's unlikely you'll be able to proceed before the traffic signals change.

Words on the road

Words painted on the road usually have a clear meaning, such as 'Stop', 'Slow' or 'Keep clear'.

When they show that a part of the road is reserved for certain types of vehicle – for example, buses, taxis or ambulances – don't park there.

Schools

Yellow zigzags are often marked on the road outside schools, along with the words 'School – keep clear'. Don't stop (even to set down or pick up children) or park there. The markings are to make sure that road users who are passing the area and children who are crossing the road have a clear, unrestricted view of the crossing area.

Destination markings

Near a busy junction, lanes sometimes have destination markings or road numbers painted on the road.

These enable road users to get into the correct lane early, even if advance direction road signs are obscured by large vehicles.

Lane arrows

These tell you which lane to take for the direction you want.

Where the road is wide enough, you may find one arrow pointing in each direction:

- left in the left-hand lane
- straight ahead in the centre lane
- right in the right-hand lane.

Some arrows might be combined, depending on how busy the junction is. If the road is only wide enough for two lanes, arrows might have two directions combined:

- straight ahead and left in the left-hand lane
- straight ahead and right in the right-hand lane.

Left- and right-turn arrows are placed well before a junction to help you get into the correct lane in good time. They don't indicate the exact point at which you should turn. It's especially important to remember this at right turns.

Speed reduction lines

Raised yellow lines may be painted across the carriageway at the approach to

- roundabouts
- reduced speed limits
- particular hazards.

The purpose of these lines is to make drivers and riders aware of their speed after a period of travelling at higher speeds. Reduce your speed in good time.

⊙→ Traffic lights

Traffic lights have three lights – red, amber and green – that change in a set cycle

- red
- red and amber together
- green
- amber
- red.

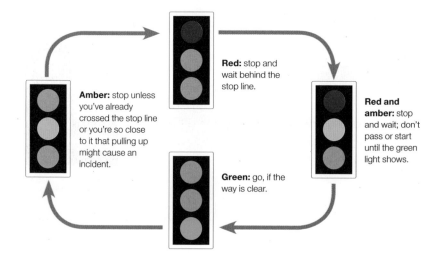

Red: stop and wait behind the stop line.

Amber: stop unless you've already crossed the stop line or you're so close to it that pulling up might cause an incident.

Red and amber: stop and wait; don't pass or start until the green light shows.

Green: go, if the way is clear.

What the colours mean

- Red – stop and wait at the stop line.
- Red and amber – stop and wait. Don't go until green shows.
- Green – go if the way is clear.
- Amber – stop, unless
    - you've already crossed the line
    - you're so close to it that pulling up might cause an incident.

Approaching traffic lights

Use the Observation – Signal – Manoeuvre (OSM) and Position – Speed – Look (PSL) routines as you approach the lights. Pay attention to lane markings and get into the correct lane in good time. Keep your speed down and be prepared to stop.

If the lights are showing green, don't speed up to 'beat the lights'. Be ready to stop, especially if the lights have been green for some time.

Green filter arrow

A green arrow in a traffic light means you can filter in the direction the arrow is pointing, even if the main light isn't showing green.

Don't enter this lane unless you want to go in the direction shown by the arrow. When turning left or right at traffic lights, take special care and give way to pedestrians already crossing.

If traffic lights fail

If the traffic lights fail, proceed with caution. Treat the situation as you would an unmarked junction.

Advance stop lines

At some traffic lights there are advance stop lines to allow cyclists to position themselves ahead of other traffic.

When the lights are amber or red, you should stop at the first white line and avoid the marked area, which is reserved for cyclists only. However, if you've crossed the first white line at the time that the signal changes to red, you must stop at the second white line even if you're in the marked area. Allow cyclists time and space to move off when the lights change to green.

In some locations there are advance areas for buses. These should be treated in the same way as those provided for cyclists.

Special traffic lights

These are often used to control traffic where low-flying aircraft pass over the road, or at swing or lifting bridges, or at other special sites such as fire stations.

Either of the following may be in operation

- normal traffic lights (red, amber and green) – follow the normal rules
- double red flashing lights – stop when the red lights are flashing.

School-crossing warning

At some busy locations, two amber lights flashing alternately warn traffic of a school crossing point ahead.

Keep your speed down and proceed with great care.

If school-crossing warning signals are flashing, you should expect the crossing to be in use and approach with care.

⊕ Traffic calming

Traffic-calming measures are used to encourage drivers and riders to travel at a lower speed than they might otherwise do. They're used in particularly sensitive areas where it's considered that a reduction in speed would benefit the immediate community.

Various features can be provided to slow down traffic, such as

- road humps
- road narrowings, central islands and chicanes
- mini-roundabouts.

20 mph zones

Some traffic-calmed areas are indicated only by a 20 mph (32 km/h) speed-limit sign.

This speed-limit sign, in addition to advising the maximum speed, indicates that there may be traffic-calming features within the signed zone; these may not be individually signed.

You should ride at a steady speed within the speed limit, and avoid frequent acceleration and deceleration within these areas.

Road humps

These may be round- or flat-topped humps laid across the carriageway. They may be used on roads where there's a speed limit of 30 mph (48 km/h) or less.

In some areas the humps are in the form of 'cushions', which cover only part of the lane and are designed so that larger vehicles, especially buses, can straddle them.

If road humps or cushions are provided outside 20 mph (32 km/h) zones, there will normally be

- warning signs at the beginning of the section of road where the hump or series of humps is installed
- triangle and edge line markings at each hump.

Road narrowings

Roads may be narrowed by the use of 'build-outs' on one or both sides of the road.

If these are provided outside 20 mph (32 km/h) zones, there will normally be

- warning signs indicating on which side of the road the narrowing occurs
- 'give way' road markings on one side of the road, accompanied by signs advising priority for oncoming vehicles.

If these are on your side of the road, you **MUST** always give way to road users approaching from the other direction.

If priority isn't given in either direction, then all road users should ensure that they can pass through the narrowing without endangering vehicles approaching from the other direction. You shouldn't accelerate as you approach the narrowing but be prepared to slow down or give way to approaching traffic.

Hold back and allow other vehicles room to pass through; don't try to squeeze through at the same time.

Mini-roundabouts

Mini-roundabouts are often used as part of traffic-calming schemes to break up a long road into shorter sections and allow traffic to join from minor roads.

Methods of dealing with mini-roundabouts are given in section 9.

Traffic calming is found in most larger towns and road-narrowing build-outs are a common feature.

You should avoid riding on the white paint at mini-roundabouts, as it can be slippery – especially when it's wet.

Psychological traffic calming

Increasingly, urban planners are choosing to remove road furniture such as kerbs, traffic lights, signs, white lines and other road markings to create 'naked roads'. The theory is that removing the sense of security provided by road furniture causes road users to exercise more caution. There's evidence that this approach reduces speed and accidents, and encourages drivers and riders to be more considerate to pedestrians.

⊕ Level crossings

At a level crossing, the road crosses railway lines. Approach and cross with care. Never

- ride onto the crossing unless the road is clear on the other side, or ride over it 'nose to tail' with another vehicle
- stop on or just after the crossing
- park close to the crossing.

Most crossings have full or half barriers, although some have no gates or barriers. If you stop at a level crossing and your wait is likely to be more than a few minutes, consider switching off your engine, as this can save fuel and cut down on pollution.

Automatic barriers

Crossings with lights
A steady amber light followed by twin flashing red lights warns of an approaching train. An audible alarm to warn pedestrians will also sound once the lights show.

You **MUST** obey the lights' signals.

Don't

- move onto the crossing after the lights show
- zigzag round half barriers
- stop on the crossing if the amber light or audible alarm starts to operate – keep going if you're already on the crossing.

131

If the train goes by and the red lights continue to flash, or the audible alarm changes tone, you **MUST** wait because another train is approaching.

Crossings without lights
At crossings with no lights, stop when the gates or barriers begin to close.

Open crossings

The sign in the shape of a cross shown in the following image is used at all level crossings without either gates or barriers.

Crossings with lights
Automatic open level crossings have flashing road traffic signals and audible warnings similar to those on crossings with barriers.

Crossings without lights
At an open crossing with no gates, barriers, attendant or traffic signals, there will be a 'give way' sign.

Look both ways, listen and make sure there's no train coming before you cross.

At an open crossing, never ride across when the lights are showing; the train can't stop for you.

User-operated crossings

These crossings are normally private and should be used by authorised users and invited guests only.

Crossings with signals

Some crossings with gates or barriers have 'stop' signs and small red and green lights. Don't cross when the red light is on because this means that a train is approaching. Cross only when the green light is on.

If you're crossing with a vehicle

• Open the gates or barriers on both sides of the crossing.

• Check the green light is still on and cross promptly.

• Close the gates or barriers when you're clear of the crossing.

Crossings without signals

Some crossings have gates but no signals. At these crossings, stop, look both ways, listen and make sure that no train is approaching.

If there's a railway telephone, you **MUST** contact the signal operator to make sure it's safe to cross.

Open the gates on both sides of the crossing and check again that no train is coming before crossing promptly.

Once you've cleared the crossing, close both gates and, if there's a telephone, inform the signal operator.

Always give way to trains – they can't stop easily.

See the Network Rail guide to using level crossings safely.

networkrail.co.uk/level-crossings

Incidents or breakdowns

If your motorcycle breaks down, or you're involved in an incident on the crossing

- Get everyone clear of the crossing.
- If there's a railway telephone, use it immediately to inform the signal operator; follow any instructions you're given.
- If there's time and if it's possible, move the motorcycle clear of the crossing.
- If the alarm sounds, or the amber light comes on, get clear of the crossing at once – the train won't be able to stop.

Crossings for trams

Look for traffic signs that show where trams cross the road. Treat them in the same way as normal railway crossings.

Take care when crossing metal rails or tramlines, particularly in wet or icy weather.

> **REMEMBER**, modern trams move quietly. Take extra care and look both ways before crossing.

Section eight
→ On the road

This section covers

- Awareness and anticipation
- Mirrors
- Rear observation
- Road position
- Stopping distance
- The road surface
- Skidding

- Separation distance
- Overtaking
- Obstructions
- Pedestrian crossings
- Tunnels
- Trams or LRT systems
- Parking

⊕ Awareness and anticipation

In any traffic situation, there are some things that are obviously going to happen and some things that **might** happen.

To anticipate is to consider and prepare for something that will or might happen.

You can anticipate what might happen by making early use of the available information on the road.

Ask yourself

- What am I likely to find?
- What are other road users trying to do?
- Should I speed up or slow down?
- Do I need to stop?

Changing and difficult conditions

Traffic conditions change constantly, so you need to

- check and recheck what's going on around you
- be alert all the time to changes in conditions, and think ahead.

How much you need to anticipate varies according to the conditions.

You'll find it more difficult to decide what might happen when

- the light is poor
- it's raining, snowy or foggy
- the traffic is heavy
- the route is unfamiliar.

Types of road

The type of road will also affect how much you can anticipate.

It's easier in light traffic to anticipate what other road users might do. It's more difficult on a busy single carriageway, dual carriageway or motorway, where there are more possibilities to consider.

Riding ahead

Look well ahead to anticipate what might happen. You need to be alert and observant at all times.

Assess the movement of all other road users, including pedestrians, as far as you can see along the stretch of road on which you're travelling.

Take in as much as possible of the road

- ahead
- behind
- to each side.

You should

- observe the middle distance and far distance, as well as the area immediately in front of you

- glance frequently in the mirrors to see what's happening in the area you've just passed
- scan the area in your view.

Observation

If you're a new rider, you'll tend to give more of your attention to controlling the motorcycle.

Practise 'reading' the road (looking for important details). You don't have to be riding to do this; you can also do it as a passenger on a motorcycle or in a car or bus. Things to look for include

- other vehicles and pedestrians
- signals given by other road users
- road signs and markings
- the type and condition of the road surface
- large vehicles, which sometimes need extra space to manoeuvre – for example, at roundabouts and other junctions
- movements of vehicles well ahead of you, as well as those immediately in front
- side roads or hills ahead
- buses signalling to move out from bus stops.

Clues

Look out for clues to help you act safely on what you see.

Watch for details in built-up areas where traffic conditions change rapidly. Be aware of the actions and reactions of other road users.

Reflections in shop windows can often give important information where vision is restricted.

A pedestrian approaching a zebra crossing might step out into the road sooner than you think.

Looking over, under and through parked vehicles may help you to see a pedestrian who is otherwise hidden from your view. This can enable you to anticipate and respond to the hazard in good time.

Take care approaching parked vehicles, especially if someone is in the driving seat.

Watch out for a driver stopping to set down or pick up a passenger. You may find they move off without warning, without checking in the mirrors or looking around.

When following a bus, watch for passengers standing up inside: the bus will probably stop shortly.

REMEMBER, try to anticipate the actions of other road users.

Be aware

How much you can see depends on how well you can see.

Your eyesight can change without you being aware of it. Have regular eyesight checks.

Your sense of hearing can also make you aware of what's happening around you. For example, if you're waiting to pull out at a junction and your view is restricted, you may hear an approaching vehicle before you can see it.

At works entrances and schools, you should expect an increased number of pedestrians, cyclists and vehicles. Watch for vehicles picking up and setting down at school start and finish times – buses as well as cars.

Emergency vehicles

Look and listen for emergency vehicles. As well as the usual emergency services – police, fire and ambulance – others, such as coastguard, bomb disposal, mountain rescue and the blood transfusion service, may use blue flashing lights. Doctors attending emergencies may use green flashing lights.

You should try to keep out of the way of any emergency vehicle. Check where they're coming from: behind (using your mirrors), ahead or across your path.

Don't panic. Watch for the path of the emergency vehicle and take any reasonable – and legal – action possible to help it get through. They won't expect you to break the law; only to make a reasonable and safe attempt to help clear the way for them so that they can do the rest.

Look well ahead and choose a sensible place to pull into the side of the road, but don't endanger yourself or other road users, or risk damage to your motorcycle.

Try to avoid stopping before the brow of a hill, a bend or a narrow section of road where the emergency vehicle may have difficulty getting through, and don't

- put yourself in a position where you would be breaking the law; for example, by crossing a red traffic light or using a bus lane during its hours of operation
- break the speed limit to get out of the way
- risk damaging your tyres, wheels or steering by riding up kerbs.

Emergency vehicles are normally travelling quickly and it's important to clear their path to allow them to do so. However, ambulances may need to travel slowly, even if they have blue lights flashing, when a patient is being treated inside. In this case, it's important for them to have a smooth ride, so don't ride in a manner that would cause the ambulance to brake or swerve sharply.

Riding in busy areas

When riding in busy areas, you should be especially alert to all possible hazards.

You should also be particularly aware of your speed and always ride at a speed appropriate to the conditions.

The speed limit is the absolute maximum and doesn't mean that it's always safe for you to ride at that speed. For example, in a narrow residential street with cars parked on either side, you'll need to ride more slowly than you would on a clear street that has the same speed limit.

 Mirrors

Mirrors must be adjusted to give a clear view behind. They should be kept clean and smear-free.

When you're riding, you might find that your elbows or shoulders obstruct the view behind. To overcome this, adjust your mirrors to the best position. If the problem remains, you may be able to solve it by fitting mirrors with longer stems.

If your mirrors vibrate, the view will be distorted. Your motorcycle dealer may be able to offer advice on how to reduce the vibration.

Using the mirrors

Glancing in your mirrors regularly will keep you up to date with the traffic situation behind. Use your mirrors before

- signalling
- changing direction
- overtaking
- changing lanes
- slowing down or stopping.

Where necessary, combine the use of your mirrors with looking behind you.

Just looking isn't enough

Whether you look in your mirrors or over your shoulder

- you must act on what you see
- think about how your actions will affect traffic behind you.

If a rider has a disability that limits the mobility/rotation of the neck, centrally mounted units that give a continuous 180-degree rear view, covering both blind spots, can be fitted centrally on the handlebars or fixed to the inside of the windscreen.

⊕ Rear observation

Rear observation refers to a combination of mirror checks and looking behind. Together, these ensure that you're always fully aware of what's happening behind you.

Before you signal, change direction or change speed, you must know how your actions will affect traffic behind you. You also need to know when traffic is likely to overtake or come alongside you.

Looking behind is important because mirrors don't give a complete view behind, leaving significant blind spots. There will be times when you need to look around to see the full picture.

Looking behind also warns other drivers that you may be about to signal or alter course.

When to look behind

Use judgement in deciding when to look behind. Obviously, when you're looking behind, you aren't looking ahead. This could be hazardous if, for example, you're close to the vehicle in front or you're overtaking at speed. Equally, there are situations when it's dangerous **not** to look behind, such as when making a right turn into a minor road.

Take rear observation when you're about to change position or speed. This might be before

- moving off
- turning left or right
- overtaking
- changing lanes
- slowing or stopping.

Warning

Looking over your shoulder too often or at the wrong moment can be hazardous. In the time you take to look behind, you

- lose touch with what's going on in front
- run the risk of veering off course.

At high speed or in congested moving traffic, your attention needs to be focused ahead. In these situations, time your rearward checks carefully.

Combine regular use of the mirrors with the lifesaver check into the blind area before altering course.

The lifesaver check

The lifesaver is a last check over your shoulder into the blind spot to make sure nothing unexpected is happening before you commit yourself to a manoeuvre.

If you're turning, use it to check the blind spot on the side you intend to turn. Use your judgement about when to use it – in congested urban situations, a lifesaver check is normally essential, especially when turning right into a minor road. However, during high-speed overtaking, when you're certain what's happening behind, it's often safer to keep your eyes on what's happening ahead.

The blind area

The blind area is the area behind and to either side of you that isn't covered by mirrors. It's very important to check for traffic in this area before

- moving off
- changing direction
- changing lane.

When checking your blind area, make sure your steering and balance aren't affected while you're looking around.

Your mirrors don't show everything that's behind you. Are you sure it's safe to manoeuvre?

⊕ Road position

Choosing your position

As a general rule, keep to the centre of your lane. On a single carriageway (two-way traffic), this means halfway between the centre of the road and the left-hand side.

Your position will depend on

- the width of the road
- the road surface

- your view ahead
- any obstructions.

Your position should allow you to

- be seen easily by traffic ahead – particularly vehicles emerging from junctions
- be seen in the mirrors of any vehicle in front
- move over to the left to create more room for oncoming traffic that's passing stationary vehicles or other obstructions.

Keep clear of the gutter, where there are often potholes and loose grit.

Avoid riding in the centre of the road. You might

- obstruct overtaking traffic
- put yourself in danger from oncoming traffic
- encourage traffic behind you to overtake on your left.

The correct position
You should always be in the correct position for the route you're going to take.

- Keep to the left if you're going straight ahead or turning left.
- Keep as close to the centre of the road as is safe when you're turning right.

Being in the correct position can help other road users to anticipate your actions.

One-way streets
Position yourself according to whether you intend to go ahead, turn left or turn right.

- To turn left, keep to the left-hand lane.
- To turn right, keep to the right-hand lane, provided there are no obstructions or parked vehicles on the right-hand side of the road you're in.
- To go ahead, be guided by the road markings. If there's no specific lane for ahead, select the most appropriate lane (normally the left-hand lane) in good time.

Follow the road markings, get into the correct lane as soon as possible and stay in that lane. Watch for drivers changing lanes suddenly.

Traffic in one-way streets often flows freely. Watch out for vehicles coming past on either side of you.

Lane discipline

You should always follow lane markings, which are there for two reasons:

- they make the best possible use of road space
- they guide the traffic.

Keeping to the lane markings is vital.

Position yourself in good time

If you find you're in the wrong lane and you don't have time to change lanes safely, carry on in your lane and find another way back to your route.

Changing lanes

Position your vehicle according to your route. Always check behind and signal in good time before you change lanes.

- Never weave from lane to lane.
- Never change lanes at the last minute.
- Always stay in the middle of your lane until you need to change.

In heavy traffic, don't obstruct 'Keep clear' markings. Look for these in congested, slow-moving traffic, especially at exits for emergency vehicles.

Allow for

- pedestrians crossing
- cyclists moving up the nearside
- large vehicles needing to straddle lanes before turning
- doors opening.

Riding ahead

Keep to the left-hand lane wherever possible. Don't use the right-hand lane just because you're travelling at speed.

On a carriageway with four or more lanes, peak-hour 'tidal flow' systems might permit or forbid use of the right-hand lanes, depending on the time of day.

Bus and cycle lanes

These are separate lanes, indicated by signs and road markings. Don't enter these lanes unless permitted by the signs.

Approaching a road junction

Look well ahead for signs and markings.

If you have two lanes in your direction and

- you intend to turn left, stay in the left-hand lane
- you intend to go ahead, stay in the left-hand lane unless otherwise indicated
- you intend to turn right, move to the right-hand lane in good time.

Don't try to gain an advantage by using an incorrect lane. Trying to change back to the proper lane at, or near, the junction is dangerous.

If you have three lanes in your direction and you intend to

- turn left, stay in the left-hand lane
- go ahead, take the left-hand lane (unless there are left filter signs) or the middle lane, or be guided by road markings
- turn right, take the right-hand lane.

Lane markings indicate the correct lane to use, but ride defensively and remember that the road markings won't be as easy to see in queuing traffic.

Slip road

Some junctions also have a slip road.

Get into the left-hand lane in good time before entering the slip road. You'll be able to use the slip road to slow down without holding up other traffic.

⊙ Stopping distance

It's important for you to know your stopping distance at all speeds. This is the distance your motorcycle travels

- from the moment you realise you must brake
- to the moment your machine stops.

Always ride so that you can stop safely within the distance you can see to be clear.

Your stopping distance depends on

- how fast you're going
- whether you're travelling uphill, on the level or downhill
- the weather and the state of the road
- the condition of your brakes and tyres
- your ability, especially your reaction times.

Stopping distance divides into thinking distance and braking distance.

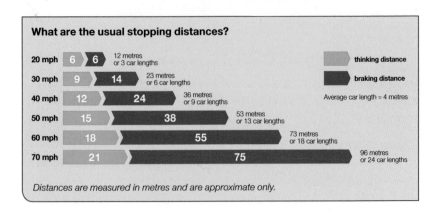

What are the usual stopping distances?

	thinking distance	braking distance	
20 mph	6	6	12 metres or 3 car lengths
30 mph	9	14	23 metres or 6 car lengths
40 mph	12	24	36 metres or 9 car lengths
50 mph	15	38	53 metres or 13 car lengths
60 mph	18	55	73 metres or 18 car lengths
70 mph	21	75	96 metres or 24 car lengths

Average car length = 4 metres

Distances are measured in metres and are approximate only.

You may be surprised to find out how much your speed affects how far you'll travel before stopping.

Thinking distance

The thinking distance is measured from the point where you see the hazard to the point where you start to brake.

This distance will vary from rider to rider and depends on reaction time. Reaction times are affected by

- age
- physical and mental condition
- health
- time of day
- use of alcohol or drugs.

An alert and fit rider needs 0.75 seconds of thinking time. This means that at 50 mph (80 km/h) you'll travel about 15 metres (about 50 feet) before you begin to brake.

Braking distance

The braking distance is measured from the point where you begin to brake to the point where you stop.

Braking distance depends on

- road conditions
- tyre condition
- brake efficiency
- suspension efficiency
- load – it takes longer to stop if you're carrying a passenger
- rider ability.

Most of all, braking distance varies with speed. At 30 mph (48 km/h) your braking distance will be about 14 metres (about 45 feet), while at 70 mph (112 km/h) this distance will increase to about 75 metres (about 245 feet).

That's just over double the speed but more than five times the braking distance.

Overall stopping distance

Your overall stopping distance is your thinking distance and braking distance combined. This increases dramatically as you increase your speed. For example, at 30 mph the overall stopping distance is 23 metres, but double your speed to 60 mph and the stopping distance increases to 73 metres – more than three times as far.

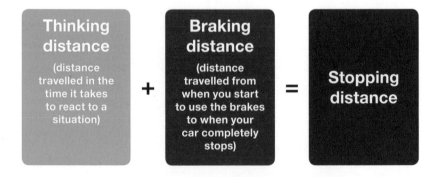

Thinking distance
(distance travelled in the time it takes to react to a situation)

+

Braking distance
(distance travelled from when you start to use the brakes to when your car completely stops)

=

Stopping distance

⊕ The road surface

The state of the road surface is very important to motorcyclists. Only a small part of the motorcycle tyre makes contact with the road, so any change in the surface can affect the stability of your motorcycle.

Be on the lookout for poor road surfaces. Beware of

- loose surfaces, such as chippings, gravel, mud and leaves
- potholes and uneven surfaces
- drain covers, especially when wet
- oil patches and spilt fuel, especially at roundabouts, bus stops and filling stations
- tar banding around road repairs
- painted road markings
- rails set into the road for trams or light rapid transit (LRT) systems. These can affect your steering and present a hazard when braking
- any shiny road surface. At junctions, frequent braking and acceleration can polish the surface.

If you can safely avoid riding on slippery surfaces, then do so. If you have to ride on a slippery surface, slow down well in advance. Don't swerve suddenly to avoid a poor surface.

If you find yourself on a slippery surface, check the traffic, then gradually slow down.

Section 12, 'All-weather riding', contains information about the effects of weather on the road surface.

⊕ Skidding

A skid is when tyres

- lose their grip on the road surface
- veer off the steered course
- reduce the effect of the brakes (by sliding over the road surface).

Causes of skidding

Skidding can be caused by a number of things, including

- heavy or uncoordinated braking, which locks one or both wheels
- excessive acceleration, causing the rear wheel to spin
- swerving (a sudden change of direction)
- leaning over too far when cornering, causing one or both tyres to lose grip.

A good rider tries to avoid skidding. The loss of control that can arise from a skid can be lethal.

Dealing with skids

Skids can happen suddenly. You need to know how to regain control when skidding occurs.

Excessive acceleration

If you've caused a skid by excessive acceleration

- The rear wheelspin can cause your machine to slide sideways. Steer in the direction that your machine is sliding.
- Ease off the throttle to regain control.

Braking

If you've caused a skid by braking

- Release the brakes to let the wheels start turning again.
- Reapply the brakes as firmly as the conditions will permit.

Your natural instinct when dealing with a skid caused by excessive braking will be to brake even harder. You must learn to overcome such instincts if you're to regain control.

Tyre grip

If your motorcycle skids when cornering or changing direction

- Steer into the skid. If the machine is sliding to the right, steer to the right. If the machine is sliding to the left, steer to the left.

- Keep your feet on the footrests. Putting your feet to the ground on a moving motorcycle could upset your balance.

New road surfaces can be very slippery, even in dry conditions, for several days after being replaced.

Separation distance

How far should you keep from the vehicle in front? Ideally, you should be no closer than the overall stopping distance that corresponds to your speed.

In heavy, slow-moving traffic, that might not be realistic, as you could be wasting valuable road space. However, even then, the gap should never be less than your thinking distance – and much more if the road is wet or slippery.

A reasonable rule to apply in good, dry conditions is a gap of one metre for each mph of your speed. For example, at 45 mph, leave a gap of 45 metres. In bad conditions, leave at least double the distance.

A useful technique for judging one metre per mph is to use the 'two-second rule'.

The two-second rule

In good, dry conditions, an alert rider, who's riding a motorcycle with good tyres and brakes, needs to be at least two seconds behind the vehicle in front.

In bad conditions, double the safety gap to four seconds or even more.

To measure this gap

Choose an obvious stationary point ahead, such as a bridge, a tree or a road sign.

In good conditions, the two-second rule is a simple yet effective way to ensure that you aren't too close to the vehicle in front.

When the vehicle in front passes the object, say to yourself 'Only a fool breaks the two-second rule.' If you reach the object before you finish saying the sentence, you're too close to the vehicle in front and need to drop back.

If another vehicle pulls into the gap you've left, ease back until you've regained your separation distance.

When a vehicle behind is following too closely, ease off the throttle very gradually and increase the gap between you and the vehicle in front. This will give you more time to react if the vehicle ahead should slow down or stop suddenly.

⊙ Overtaking

The size, manoeuvrability and acceleration rate of a motorcycle give riders better opportunities to overtake slower-moving vehicles than are available to car drivers.

However, overtaking can put you on a collision course with traffic from the opposite direction, and it's one of the main causes of road traffic incidents. Overtaking at the wrong time or in the wrong place is extremely dangerous. It's vital to choose your time and place carefully.

Overtaking a moving vehicle

Before you overtake, ask yourself whether it's really necessary. If you decide it is, you need to find a suitable place.

You **MUST NOT** overtake where to do so would cause you to break the law. Details are shown in The Highway Code.

In addition, some places are never suitable. For example, **don't** overtake

- if your view ahead is blocked
- if there's too little room
- if the road narrows
- if you're approaching a bend or junction
- if there's 'dead ground' – a dip in the road that might hide an oncoming vehicle.

Steps to overtaking

You might need to follow some or all of these steps several times before the right moment arrives. For example, if someone overtakes you just as you're about to overtake, you'll need to start all over again.

Use the OSM/PSL routine:

O – Observation Check your mirrors/look around to assess the situation behind and look well ahead.

S – Signal Give a signal if it will help

- drivers behind
- the driver you're overtaking
- drivers coming towards you.

M – Manoeuvre Use the PSL routine:

P – Position Be near enough to the vehicle ahead to overtake smoothly when you're ready, but not so close that you can't get a good view of the road ahead.

S – Speed You need enough reserve power to go past briskly. You might need to change down so that you can accelerate swiftly when you're ready to start overtaking.

L – Look Assess the whole situation, including

- the state of the road
- what the driver ahead is doing or might be about to do
- any hazards
- the speed and position of oncoming vehicles
- the speed difference between you and oncoming vehicles.

Make a final check in front and behind. Be aware of, and check, any blind spots by taking a quick sideways glance if necessary before deciding to pull out to overtake. If it's safe, pull out on a smooth, easy line, then

- overtake as quickly as you can
- move back to the left again on a smooth, easy line, but avoid cutting in.

Never begin to overtake if another vehicle is overtaking you or is about to do so.

Overtake only when you're sure it's safe to do so.

> **REMEMBER**, if you're travelling at high speed, it's safer to combine regular use of the mirrors with the lifesaver check before changing course.

Before overtaking

Many danger spots are marked with double white lines along the road. Look out for arrows warning you to move over to the left as you're approaching these areas.

Junction signs and hatch markings in the middle of the road are warnings not to overtake. Be ready to hold back in case traffic is waiting to turn right or slowing to turn left.

Watch the vehicle in front
Before overtaking, decide what the driver in front is likely to do by watching both them and the road ahead for a while. They might

- decide to overtake
- continue to drive at the speed of the vehicle ahead of them
- intend to turn off soon
- have seen something ahead that you haven't.

Vehicles turning right
Research has shown that most overtaking incidents are caused by the overtaking driver or rider hitting a vehicle that's turning right. To avoid this type of collision, you should

- consciously check the indicators of the vehicle you're about to overtake
- assume that a vehicle that's slowing down is about to turn.

Following through
Never automatically follow an overtaking vehicle without being able to see for yourself that the way is clear. The vehicle in front obscures your view and hides you from the view of oncoming traffic.

Always make your own decisions about overtaking, based on what **you** see and what **you** know.

Be patient. If in doubt, hold back.

Defensive riding

Keep well back from any vehicle that's too close to the vehicle in front and swinging in and out. Be patient, in case the driver does something hasty.

Judging speed and distance

The speed of the vehicle you're overtaking is very important. When you're closing up behind a moving vehicle, it will cover quite a distance before you can actually pass it – probably much more than you think.

For example, if you're riding at 30 mph (48 km/h), it could take a quarter of a mile (400 metres) just to catch up with a vehicle 200 yards (180 metres) ahead that's travelling at 15 mph (24 km/h).

On the other hand, if you're riding at 55 mph (88.5 km/h) and an oncoming vehicle is doing the same, you're actually approaching each other at 110 mph (177 km/h) or 50 metres per second.

Overtaking takes time. The smaller the difference between your speed and the speed of the vehicle you're overtaking, the longer the stretch of clear road you'll need.

Defensive riding

Never accelerate when someone is overtaking you. Be prepared to ease off, if necessary, to help them pass you.

Overtaking large vehicles

If you're considering overtaking a large vehicle, you need to keep well back to ensure that you

* have the best view of the road ahead
* allow the driver of the large vehicle to see you in their mirrors.

> **REMEMBER**, if you can't see the vehicle's mirrors, the driver can't see you. Be especially aware that left-hand-drive vehicles have different blind spots from those of right-hand-drive vehicles.

Leave a good space while waiting to overtake. If another vehicle fills the gap, drop back again.

Also, note whether the vehicle you intend to overtake is loaded or unloaded. The speed of large vehicles varies greatly when they're going up and down hills. A loaded vehicle might crawl slowly uphill and then pick up speed surprisingly quickly on the downhill run. Always remember these possible changes in speed when you're thinking of overtaking.

Avoid riding alongside large vehicles, because the driver may not be able to see you if you're in a blind spot.

Overtaking slow-moving vehicles

You may encounter several types of slow-moving vehicle on the roads. These include farm machinery, tractors, roadworks vehicles and refuse collection vehicles. Most will have flashing amber beacons.

Tractors and farm machinery will often pull in to the left when it's safe, or if there's space to do so, to let a queue of traffic pass. However, they aren't always able to do so.

It can be frustrating to be travelling behind a slow-moving vehicle, but be patient. Wait until the road ahead is completely clear of oncoming traffic and you're sure it's both safe and legal to overtake. Remember also that there may be workers in the road – for example, around roadworks vehicles or refuse collection trucks.

Don't overtake

* on the approach to a bend
* before the brow of a hill
* where there's a dip in the road ahead that could hide an oncoming vehicle.

In rural areas, there may be entrances to farm properties where vehicles may emerge.

Only overtake if your view of the road ahead is completely clear and unobstructed, and you're sure there's no oncoming traffic. Also check behind to make sure no other vehicle is trying to overtake at the same time.

Leave plenty of room when overtaking and allow plenty of time for your manoeuvre. Some vehicles, especially those towing farm machinery, may be wider or longer than expected.

Overtaking on a hill

Uphill
Give yourself time and room to return to your side of the road well before the brow of the hill. Your zone of vision will get shorter as you approach the brow of the hill. Don't forget that oncoming vehicles will be travelling downhill and could be approaching very quickly.

Downhill
It's more difficult to slow down when going downhill. If you overtake going downhill, you may find yourself travelling faster than you intended. Be careful not to lose control of your motorcycle.

Overtaking on long hills
On some long hills, double white lines divide the road so that there are two lanes for traffic going uphill, but only one downhill.

If the line is broken on the downhill side, this means you can overtake going downhill if it's safe to do so.

Overtaking on three-lane roads

Some roads are divided into three lanes, where the middle lane can be used for overtaking in either direction. These roads can be particularly dangerous. Before overtaking, you must make sure the road is clear far enough ahead. If in doubt, **wait**.

Some three-lane roads have double white lines marked on the road to allow vehicles travelling uphill to overtake.

Overtaking on the left

You should never overtake on the left unless

- the vehicle in front is signalling to turn right, and you can safely pass on the left. Take care if there's a road to the left; oncoming traffic turning right into it may be hidden by the vehicle you're overtaking
- traffic is moving slowly in queues, and vehicles in the lane on your right are moving more slowly than you are.

Passing on the left

In addition, you can go past on the inside of slower traffic when

- you're in a one-way street (but not a dual carriageway) where vehicles are allowed to pass on either side
- you're in the correct lane to turn left at a junction.

Overtaking on dual carriageways

Overtake only if you're sure you can do so safely.

You should normally stay in the left-hand lane and only use the right-hand lane for overtaking or turning right. If you use the right-hand lane for overtaking, you should move back to the left-hand lane as soon as it's safe to do so.

Plan well ahead and use the appropriate parts of the OSM/PSL routine. For example

Observation Use your mirrors/rear observation to assess the speed and position of following traffic. On a high-speed dual carriageway, start the checks in plenty of time.

Signal Give a signal if it will help the driver you're overtaking and other drivers further ahead. Be aware that on a dual carriageway, a vehicle in the right lane signalling right may be slowing to turn right through the central reservation.

Manoeuvre This is broken down into three stages:

Position Keep well back from the vehicle you're going to overtake, so that you have a good view of the road ahead.

Speed Make sure you have enough speed in reserve to overtake briskly, without breaking any speed limits.

Look Look ahead and assess

* the condition of the road
* what the vehicle ahead is doing
* any hazards.

Check behind again to reassess the situation. Don't begin to overtake if another vehicle is about to overtake you.

Overtake briskly, then make sure you're well clear of the vehicle you've overtaken before moving back to the left. Don't cut in.

Overtaking on the left
You mustn't overtake on the left unless traffic is moving slowly in queues, and the queue on your right is moving more slowly than you are.

Never move to a lane on your left to overtake.

Defensive riding
Be considerate. Don't block faster vehicles that might want to overtake you, even if they're breaking the speed limit.

Vulnerable road users

Allow plenty of room
When overtaking cyclists, other motorcyclists or horse riders, make sure you give them plenty of room. Never attempt to overtake them just before you turn left or if you would have to stop or slow down soon afterwards.

If they look over their shoulder, it could mean that they intend to pull out, turn right or change direction. Give them time and space to do so.

Before overtaking, you must be certain that you can return to your side of the road safely without getting in the way of

* vehicles coming towards you
* vehicles you're overtaking.

Filtering

The small size of a motorcycle makes it possible to filter through slow or stationary queues of traffic. Filtering requires great care and can expose you to additional hazards. You must comply with The Highway Code.

Before you begin to filter, you need to think about

- whether there's enough space for you to filter through safely. Identify a place where you can rejoin the traffic flow before you move out
- choosing an appropriate speed to give yourself – and others – time to react.

You should consider the actions of other road users at all times and be on the lookout for

- the angled wheels and flashing indicators that suggest a vehicle is about to change lanes
- pedestrians and cyclists
- vehicles emerging or turning at junctions
- doors opening suddenly
- other motorcyclists filtering

- areas of the road surface that have less grip or could upset your balance; for example, white paint and road studs.

Be ready to brake and/or use the horn if you don't think you've been seen.

> **REMEMBER**, other road users may not be expecting a filtering motorcycle. Make yourself easy to see by wearing bright clothing and use your headlights on dipped beam.

⮕ Obstructions

The way to deal with any obstruction is to look and plan well ahead, and to use the OSM/PSL routine.

The decision to wait or to go around the obstruction will depend on

- the type and width of the road
- whether the obstruction is on
    - your side of the road
    - the other side of the road
    - both sides of the road
- whether there's approaching traffic
- the behaviour of following road users
- the room available.

If you have to stop and wait, keep well back from the obstruction, in a position that not only keeps your zone of vision open but also doesn't impede the approaching traffic.

As a general rule, if the obstruction is on your side of the road, approaching traffic will have priority.

Don't assume that you have priority if the obstruction is on the other side of the road. Always be prepared to give way and remember that the obstruction could conceal something, such as a pedestrian.

Procedure

Look well ahead to identify the obstruction in good time before using the OSM/PSL routine.

Observation Use your mirrors. Take rear observation if necessary.

Signal Signal if necessary.

Position Decide on your position. Avoid keeping so far to the left that you have to steer past the obstruction at the last minute; a gradual change of course is required.

Speed Adjust your speed as necessary. This will depend on the situation, but aim to regulate your speed to take a smooth and steady course without stopping.

Look Finally, look and assess the situation before you decide whether it's necessary to wait or safe to proceed.

Obstructions on hills

These need special care. Give yourself the time and space you need, remembering that you may need to brake earlier than normal.

If you're travelling downhill and the obstruction is on the other side of the road, don't take your priority for granted. If it's safe, be prepared to give way to traffic coming uphill, especially heavy vehicles. Your consideration will be appreciated.

Roadworks

These areas make the usable width of the road much narrower. They can be controlled either by temporary traffic lights or by workers with stop/go boards. Watch out for temporary road surfaces or debris on the road.

Obey all lights and signs, slow down and look out for workers who may be walking on or near the road.

If you need to pass an obstruction, make sure you can see that it's safe. Don't blindly follow the vehicle in front.

Defensive riding

Don't follow through behind the vehicle in front without being able to see for yourself that the way ahead is clear.

Keep a safe distance from the obstruction and the approaching traffic. Where space is limited, reduce your speed and take extra care. The smaller the gap, the lower your speed needs to be.

⊕ Pedestrian crossings

The rider and pedestrian crossings

People on foot have certain rights of way at pedestrian crossings.

Some rules and advice apply to all types of crossing.

- You **MUST NOT** park
    - on a crossing; this blocks the way for pedestrians
    - within the area marked by zigzag lines; this obstructs both the pedestrians' view of approaching vehicles and approaching drivers' view of the crossing.

- You **MUST NOT** overtake
    - the moving vehicle nearest to a crossing
    - the leading vehicle that has stopped to give way to a pedestrian.
- Even if there are no zigzag lines, never overtake just before a crossing.
- Give yourself more time to stop if the road is wet or icy.
- Keep crossings clear when queuing in traffic, stopping before the crossing if you can see that you won't be able to clear it.
- Always allow pedestrians plenty of time to cross, especially if they're older or disabled. Don't try to hurry them by revving your engine or edging forward.
- Watch out for pedestrians who try to rush across at the last minute.

Also, on all signal-controlled crossings you should

- give way to anyone still on the crossing even if the signal for vehicles has changed to green
- proceed with extreme caution if the signals aren't working.

> **REMEMBER**, you should take extra care where the view of either side of the crossing is blocked by queuing traffic. Pedestrians may be crossing between these vehicles, incorrectly thinking they've stopped to allow them to cross.

Additional rules for different types of crossing

Zebra crossings

Zebra crossings have flashing yellow beacons on both sides of the road and black-and-white stripes on the crossing. They also have white zigzag markings on both sides of the crossing and a 'give way' line about a metre from the crossing, which marks the place for drivers and riders to stop when necessary. When pedestrians are waiting to cross at a zebra crossing, check your mirrors and stop if you can do so safely.

The flashing yellow beacons at some zebra crossings can be difficult to see in bright sunshine.

> **REMEMBER**, some zebra crossings are divided by a central island. Each half is a separate crossing.

Be aware also of pedestrians approaching the crossing. They may suddenly start to move onto the crossing, so be ready to stop for them.

You **MUST** give way to anyone who

- is already crossing
- has stepped onto the crossing.

Don't wave people across. There could be another vehicle coming in the other direction and you can't be sure what other drivers or riders might do.

Pelican crossings

These are light-controlled crossings where the pedestrian uses push-button controls to control the lights. They have no red-and-amber phase before the green light. Instead, they

At a pelican crossing, the amber light flashes to give pedestrians enough time to finish crossing before the lights change to green.

have a flashing amber light, which means you must give way to pedestrians on the crossing but may drive across if the crossing is clear.

The crossing area is shown by studs and a 'stop' line marks the place for drivers and riders to stop when it's necessary.

Pelican crossings may be

- straight – a pelican crossing that goes straight across the road is one crossing, even if there's a central refuge. You must wait for people coming from the other side of the refuge
- staggered – if the crossings on each side of the central refuge aren't in line, the crossings are separate.

Puffin crossings

These are user-friendly, 'intelligent' crossings where electronic devices automatically detect when pedestrians are on the crossing and delay the green light until the pedestrians have reached a position of safety.

At a puffin crossing, there's no flashing amber phase and the lights follow the normal traffic-light sequence.

Unnecessary delays in traffic flow are reduced by these devices.

- If the pedestrians cross quickly, the pedestrian phase is shortened.
- If the pedestrians have crossed the road before the phase starts, it will automatically be cancelled.

The light sequence at these crossings is the same as at traffic lights (see section 7).

Toucan crossings

These are shared by pedestrians and cyclists. Cyclists are permitted to cycle across.

The light sequence at these crossings is the same as at traffic lights.

Equestrian crossings

These are for horse riders and may be alongside those for pedestrians and cyclists. They have wider crossing areas, pavement barriers and either one or two sets of controls, one being set at a higher position.

*You **MUST** obey signals given by a school crossing patrol.*

School crossing patrols

Watch out for these patrols and obey their signals.

At particularly dangerous locations, two amber lights flashing alternately give advance warning of the crossing point.

Don't overtake when you're approaching a school crossing. Always keep your speed down so you're ready to slow down or stop if necessary.

Defensive riding

Always look well ahead to identify pedestrian crossings early. Look for the flashing yellow beacons, traffic lights, zigzag markings, etc.

Use the OSM/PSL routine and keep your speed down.

Brake lights can't be seen by the pedestrians at the crossing or by approaching traffic, so if you're the leading vehicle you should consider using an arm signal when you're slowing down or stopping at a zebra crossing.

⊕ Tunnels

When approaching a tunnel

- Stop and remove any sunglasses or sun visor.
- Make sure you use your dipped headlights.
- Observe the road signs and signals.
- Keep an appropriate distance from the vehicle in front.

When entering a tunnel, your visibility will be suddenly reduced. Be prepared for this change in conditions and make sure that you can stop within the distance you can see to be clear. Increase the distance between you and the vehicle in front if necessary.

If the tunnel is congested

- Switch on your hazard warning lights. Only use them for long enough to ensure that your warning has been seen.
- Keep your distance, even if you're moving slowly or have stopped.
- If possible, listen out for messages on the radio.
- Follow any instructions given by tunnel officials or variable message signs.

For action to take in the event of a breakdown or road traffic incident, see section 16.

If it's a sunny day, make allowances for the lower light level as you enter a tunnel and be prepared for the dazzle of bright sunshine as you emerge.

⊙ Trams or LRT systems

Light rapid transit (LRT) systems, or 'metros', are being introduced in many large towns and cities to provide a more efficient and environmentally friendly form of public transport.

Tram systems are common throughout Europe and there are plans to introduce them to more cities in the UK.

Trams may operate completely separately from other traffic or they may run on roads open to other traffic. As they run on rails, they're fixed in the route they follow and can't manoeuvre around other road users. The vehicles may run singly or as multiple units, and may be up to 60 metres (about 200 feet) long. Remember that trams are quiet, move quickly and can't steer to avoid you.

The area occupied by a tram is marked by paving or markings on the road surface. This 'swept path' must always be kept clear. Anticipate well ahead and never stop on or across the tracks or markings except when in queuing traffic or at traffic lights.

Take extra care when you first encounter trams until you're accustomed to dealing with the different traffic system.

Crossing points

Deal with these in exactly the same way as normal railway crossings.

Also bear in mind the speed and silent approach of trams.

Reserved areas

Drivers mustn't enter 'reserved areas' for the trams, which are marked with white line markings, a different type of surface, or both.

The reserved areas are usually one-way, but may sometimes be two-way.

Hazards

The steel rails can be slippery whether it's wet or dry. Try to avoid riding on the rails and take extra care when braking or turning on them, to avoid the risk of skidding.

Take care also where

- the tracks run close to the kerb to pick up or set down passengers
- the lines move from one side of the road to the other.

Tram stops

Where a tram stops at a platform, either in the middle or at the side of the road, follow the route shown by road signs and markings. If there's no passing lane signed, wait behind the tram until it moves off.

At stops without platforms, don't ride between a tram and the left-hand kerb when a tram has stopped to pick up or set down passengers.

Warning signs and signals

Obey all warning signs or signals controlling traffic. Where there are no signals, always give way to trams.

Diamond-shaped signs or white light signals give instructions to tram drivers only.

Do

- watch out for additional pedestrian crossings where passengers will be getting on and off the trams. You must stop for them
- make allowances for other road users who may not be familiar with tram systems
- be especially aware of the dangers of tram rails for cyclists, motorcyclists and moped riders. Narrow tyres can slip or even become trapped when they come into contact with the rails.

Don't

- try to race a tram where there isn't enough road space for both vehicles side by side; remember the end of the vehicle swings out on bends
- overtake at tram stops
- ride between platforms at tramway stations. Follow the direction signs
- park so that your vehicle obstructs the trams or would force other drivers to do so. Remember that a tram can't steer round an obstruction.

⊙ Parking

The parking rules in The Highway Code also apply to motorcycles. When you park, take care to

- park on firm, level ground. The motorcycle's stand can sink into soft ground, causing the machine to fall over. On a very hot day, side or centre stands can sink into tarmac softened by the heat. If your machine falls over, it could injure a passer-by or damage another parked vehicle
- use the centre stand if you're leaving your machine for some time
- switch off the fuel tap (if fitted)
- lock the steering and take the ignition key with you.

If you park a sidecar outfit on a gradient, make sure that it doesn't roll away. Leave the machine in a low gear and block a wheel or wedge it against the kerb.

You mustn't park in parking bays reserved for residents, or for vehicles belonging to disabled people, unless you're permitted to do so.

Motorcycle parking places

In many towns you can find areas set aside for motorcycle parking. These areas sometimes have fixed metal stands to which you can secure your motorcycle.

Some car parks also set aside areas for motorcycles. Look for signs or marked-out parking bays.

> **Many local government websites carry information on where to park.**

Security

Theft of motorcycles is all too common, but you can take steps to make it more difficult for thieves.

- If possible, park in a car park displaying the Park Mark® Safer Parking logo. These car parks have been approved by the police. They make sure that the site has measures in place to create a safe environment.
- If parking on the road during the day, park in a busy public place.
- At night, park in a well-lit area.
- Try not to park in the same place every day.
- Don't leave your helmet or other possessions with the motorcycle.

When securing your motorcycle, always use the steering lock. Additional locking devices include a high-tension steel cable or chain with a high-quality padlock, a U-lock or a disc lock.

Fastening your motorcycle to an immovable object or another motorcycle will give extra security.

To find your nearest Park Mark® awarded site, visit

parkmark.co.uk

and enter your postcode into the search box.

Other security measures

In addition to locking up your motorcycle, you may use other security measures.

These include

- fitting an alarm – make sure the alarm is suitable for your machine. It's a good idea to display a sticker warning that the motorcycle is protected by an alarm – but not the alarm make or model
- having your motorcycle security marked – this involves having the Vehicle Identification Number (VIN) put on the motorcycle. This is unobtrusive, and having it put on as many parts as possible will, in the event of theft, help the police to return the motorcycle.

REMEMBER, lock it or lose it!

Parking for disabled riders

Disabled riders who qualify for the Blue Badge parking scheme can use designated disabled parking bays, as long as the badge is clearly displayed on the vehicle.

Blue Badges can be a target for thieves, so try to make sure that your badge is secured to your vehicle. If you need additional help and advice, the National Association of Disabled Bikers runs a secure badge holder scheme. Visit **nabd.org.uk** for more information.

→ Bends and junctions

This section covers

- Bends
- Junctions
- The junction routine
- Turning
- Emerging
- Types of junction
- Roundabouts
- Junctions on dual carriageways

⊕ Bends

Modern roads present a huge variety of bends, corners and junctions – points where the road changes direction.

These are often major hazards, and accident statistics show that no rider can afford to venture out without a thorough knowledge of how to deal with them. The whole of this section is devoted to dealing with bends, corners and junctions safely.

Dealing effectively with bends demands that you look well ahead and make an accurate assessment of how severe the bend is and at what speed you need to be travelling to negotiate it safely.

> **REMEMBER**, a bend can feel like a sharp corner if you approach it too fast, and you'll find it more difficult to keep your motorcycle under control.

Assessing bends

Look ahead

Look well ahead for any indications, such as road signs, warnings and road markings, which will tell you

- the type of bend
- the direction the road takes
- how sharp the bend is
- whether the bend is one of a series.

Assess the situation

Ask yourself

- How dangerous does it seem? Remember, if the word 'slow' is painted on the road, that means there's a hazard and you need to respond to it safely.
- What if there's an obstruction on the bend, such as a slow-moving or parked vehicle?

- Are there likely to be pedestrians on your side of the road? Is there a footpath?

- Is there an adverse camber? Remember that on a right-hand bend an adverse camber could make your motorcycle veer to the left.

Always ride so you can stop safely within the limit of your vision. Where your view is restricted, adjust your speed accordingly.

Limit points

Understanding limit points, and learning how to use them to improve your riding ability, is an important skill to master.

Simply put, the limit point is the furthest uninterrupted view of the road surface ahead, or the point at which the two verges – left and right – appear to meet.

If the limit point is rushing towards you, then you should slow down and allow yourself more time and space in which to stop.

If the limit point appears to be a constant distance away from you, this indicates that your speed on approach to the bend is correct, providing you can still stop in the distance you can see to be clear.

If the limit point is moving away from you, this indicates that you may start to accelerate as the bend opens out.

The following diagram illustrates the point.

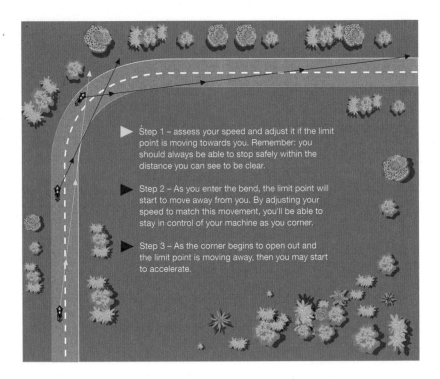

Step 1 – assess your speed and adjust it if the limit point is moving towards you. Remember: you should always be able to stop safely within the distance you can see to be clear.

Step 2 – As you enter the bend, the limit point will start to move away from you. By adjusting your speed to match this movement, you'll be able to stay in control of your machine as you corner.

Step 3 – As the corner begins to open out and the limit point is moving away, then you may start to accelerate.

Counter-steering

When a motorcycle is travelling at more than a walking pace, the rider can use a method of steering known as 'counter-steering' or 'positive steering'. This may seem unusual at first. However, once you have an understanding of how the method works, it's simple and effective.

To turn left, simply push lightly on the left grip. To turn right, push lightly on the right grip.

This initial push on the grip is the first part of a process of balancing and steering the motorcycle. The input is called counter-steering because you momentarily steer the front wheel opposite, or counter to, the direction you want to go. Doing this will cause the machine to lean into the bend in the direction of travel.

Once the correct lean angle for the bend has been reached, you should allow the steering to realign itself by releasing the steering input or pressure. Using a constant amount of throttle will help to stabilise the machine throughout the corner.

If necessary, you can further control the direction of the motorcycle by making small adjustments to steering. To turn a little more tightly, push the grip a little further towards the curve.

Your speed, position and gear should be correct before you start to turn.

REMEMBER, it's important to get advice from a motorcycle trainer to help you learn to counter-steer safely.

Negotiating bends

Approach with care

- As you approach, use the Observation – Signal – Manoeuvre (OSM)/ Position – Speed – Look (PSL) routine.

- Before you reach the bend, take up the best approach position for the type of bend. Adjust your speed, if necessary, and select the most suitable gear.

Entering the bend

As you enter the bend, use the throttle just enough to keep

- the tyres gripping

- full control.

After you begin to turn

Avoid braking, except in an emergency.

Right-hand bends

Keep to the left to improve your view, but don't move too far to the left if this would put you at risk. Watch out for

- drains, gravel and road debris
- uneven or slippery surfaces
- drives, entrances, junctions and exits
- road junctions
- adverse camber.

When riding around a right-hand bend, don't ride too close to the centre line. You may enter the other side of the road as you bank, putting yourself in the path of oncoming traffic.

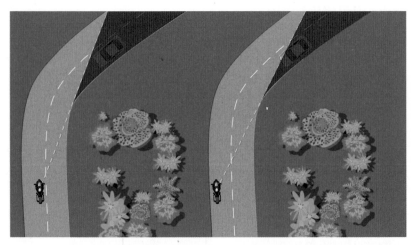

On a right-hand bend, keeping to the left may improve your view – but watch out for hazards.

Left-hand bends

As you approach a left-hand bend, you should generally keep to your normal riding position. You can consider moving out to the centre of the road if it's safe to do so, as this may give you an improved view. If you do this, you should bear in mind that it may place you too close to oncoming traffic or mislead other road users.

The road camber may work to your advantage, but don't go too fast.

In particular, look out for

- pedestrians, especially when there's no footpath
- horse riders
- stationary or broken-down vehicles
- oncoming vehicles crossing the centre line
- vehicles waiting to turn right.

On a left-hand bend, moving towards the centre of the road may improve your view – but don't put yourself at risk.

Be prepared to change your position if necessary; for example, if there's a diesel spill or an obstruction in the road.

Always ride at such a speed that you can stop safely in the distance you can see to be clear.

Camber

The camber of a road is the angle at which the road slopes away from the centre to help drainage.

On a left-hand bend, the road usually slopes down in the same direction as the turn. This increases the effect of your steering.

On a right-hand bend, the road normally slopes down in the opposite direction to the turn. This reduces the effect of your steering.

Adverse camber
Here the road slopes downwards towards the outside of the corner and the forces acting on your motorcycle could cause it to leave the road more easily than on a normal corner.

Banking
On a few bends, such as some motorway slip roads, the road slopes upwards towards the outside of the bend. This applies across the whole width of the road, but here traffic is usually restricted to travelling in one direction only.

A road surface that slopes down to the inside of a bend helps cornering.

A road surface that slopes up to the inside of a bend makes cornering more difficult.

Speed

Judging the correct road speed as you approach bends and corners takes practice and experience. Make sure you're going at the right speed to negotiate the bend safely.

That speed will depend on the

- type and condition of the road
- sharpness of the bend
- camber of the road
- visibility
- weather conditions.

Adjusting your speed

Reduce speed before you enter the bend.

The correct speed is the one that takes your motorcycle around the bend under full control, with the greatest safety for you, your passenger and other road users.

You can reduce your speed by rolling off the throttle and

- allowing your road speed to fall
- using the brakes progressively and, if necessary, changing to a lower gear.

Your speed should be at its lowest as you begin to turn.

Gears

Make sure you select the correct gear before you enter the bend. The correct gear will depend on a number of factors, including

* your speed
* the road conditions
* other traffic
* warning signs and road markings.

Using the throttle

Don't confuse 'using the throttle' with 'accelerating', which means going faster. When dealing with bends, 'using the throttle' means using it just enough to make the engine drive the motorcycle around the bend.

As you leave the bend and can see further ahead, you can increase your speed to suit the road and traffic conditions.

Caution
Too much throttle can cause the rear tyre to lose grip and skid.

Braking on a bend

Avoid braking on a bend. If you must brake on a bend

* try to avoid using the front brake. Rely on the rear brake and engine braking to slow you down. If you must use the front brake, be very gentle. There's a risk of the front tyre losing its grip and sliding sideways
* try to bring your motorcycle upright and brake normally (provided you can do so safely).

Stopping on a bend

Avoid stopping on a bend, except in an emergency. If you have to stop, either

* get your motorcycle off the road, or

- stop where following traffic can see you. This is especially important on left-hand bends, where vision can be more limited.

If you can, stop clear of a continuous centre line.

A series of bends

Double and multiple bends are almost always signed. Take note of

- road signs
- double white lines
- arrows directing you to move to the left.

For example, if the second bend follows closely after the first and you haven't taken notice of the road signs or markings, you could find yourself speeding up when you should be slowing down.

On a winding road, selecting the appropriate gear will help you to

- ride at a safe speed
- keep the right amount of load on the engine and the right amount of grip on the road.

Where there's a series of bends, they often turn in alternate directions. As soon as you've negotiated one, you have to prepare for the next. Look well ahead for changes in the camber of the road, which could affect your control.

At night

On unfamiliar roads, the lights of oncoming traffic may help you to plan ahead. However, negotiating bends at night has its own hazards.

- Anticipate hazards around the bend.
- Be prepared to be affected by the lights of oncoming traffic, especially on right-hand bends. Don't be taken by surprise.
- Dip your headlights in advance for oncoming traffic approaching the bend, especially on left-hand bends.

Load

Any change in the centre of gravity of the motorcycle or the weight it's carrying will affect its handling on bends, compared with when it's lightly loaded.

This change may be caused by

- a pillion passenger
- carrying heavy objects
- incorrect tyre pressure.

Defensive riding

Always be on the lookout for other vehicles creating dangerous situations, such as

- a vehicle overtaking too close to a bend
- a vehicle approaching a bend too fast
- oncoming vehicles straddling the centre lines
- oncoming vehicles skidding in bad weather
- a vehicle waiting to turn into a concealed entrance.

⊙ Junctions

A junction is a point where two or more roads meet. Junctions are hazards, where there's a significant risk of an incident occurring. Treat them with great care, no matter how easy they look.

Advance information

Look for information about the junction ahead, and the level of difficulty, such as

- the type of junction
- the amount of traffic

- warning signs
- road markings
- direction signs
- 'give way' and 'stop' signs
- traffic lights
- a break in the line of buildings
- changes in road surface.

Approaching junctions

The way you approach a junction depends on what you intend to do. You might want to

- cross a major road going ahead
- emerge into a major road by turning right
- emerge into a major road by turning left
- leave a major road by turning right or left into a minor road
- stay on a major road and pass the junction.

A major road is one with priority over another at a junction.

Priority

Usually, road signs and markings indicate priority. Where no priority is shown at a junction, take care and don't rush.

Lanes at junctions

When you approach a junction

- do so in the correct lane for the direction you intend to take
- look well ahead and watch for traffic and direction signs
- look out for signals from vehicles about to change lanes
- look out for vehicles suddenly changing lanes without signalling.

Articulated or long vehicles

Stay clear of large vehicles at junctions. They need much more room than smaller vehicles and may be in a position that seems incorrect to you.

The driver often needs to straddle lanes, swing out to the right before turning left, or swing to the left before turning right. Don't be tempted to squeeze past at junctions and roundabouts. The rear wheels might cut across your path as the vehicle turns.

Be ready for them to stop if their way is blocked.

Approaching minor roads

Look out for road signs indicating minor roads, even if you aren't turning off. Be cautious if you see a 'keep clear' road marking, as traffic could be emerging and may not see you.

Watch out for emerging vehicles; the driver's view is often reduced at narrow junctions and they might pull out in front of you. See section 10 for more information.

If this happens, and you aren't sure that the driver has seen you, slow down. Consider altering your position and be prepared to stop.

Even if a waiting driver appears to have seen you, ride defensively and be prepared to stop if necessary.

REMEMBER, don't overtake at, or approaching, a junction.

The road surface at junctions

Always watch out for slippery surfaces or loose chippings. Avoid braking while you're turning. Plan ahead – brake before the junction.

Defensive riding

Adjust your overall speed when passing a series of minor roads so you can stop within the distance you can see to be clear.

⊙ The junction routine

At every junction, use the OSM/PSL routine.

Observation Take effective observation. Use your mirrors and look round if necessary to make sure you know what's happening behind you.

Signal Signal clearly and in good time.

Manoeuvre Use the PSL routine:

Position If the road has no lane markings

- when turning left, keep to the left
- when turning right, keep as close to the centre of the road as is safe. In a one-way street, move to the right-hand side of the road in good time.

If the road has lane markings

- use the correct lane for the direction you intend to take
- move into the lane as soon as you can.

Speed Adjust your speed as necessary.

Look Watch for other traffic when you reach a point from which you can see.

The junction routine should enable you to cope with all likelihoods at road junctions.

When you're moving ahead

* make sure that you're in the correct lane
* look out for vehicles changing lane, either with or without signalling.

 Turning

Turning right into a side road

Assess the junction and use the OSM/PSL routine. Check the road signs and markings.

Observation Look in your mirrors and take rear observation as necessary.

Signal Signal right in good time.

Manoeuvre Use the PSL routine:

Position Make sure you're safe by checking the mirrors and looking behind as necessary, then position yourself as close to the centre of the road as is safe, so that vehicles can pass on your left. In a one-way street, keep to the right-hand side of the road.

Speed Adjust your speed as necessary. Watch out for approaching traffic. Stop if necessary.

Look Look into the road you're joining. Watch for vehicles waiting to emerge and pedestrians crossing the road.

Take a lifesaver glance over your right shoulder just before you turn. Do this early enough for you to change your plan if it isn't safe to turn.

Avoid cutting the corner (enter on the left-hand side of the road).

When you've completed the turn

* Cancel your signal.
* Check for traffic behind you.
* Accelerate progressively to a speed suitable for the road and traffic conditions, within the set speed limit.

Turning left into a side road

Assess the junction and use the OSM/PSL routine. Check the road signs and markings.

Observation Generally, a well-timed look in the mirrors is enough to see what's going on behind you before you signal. Sometimes you might consider taking a lifesaver glance as well.

Signal Signal left at the correct time.

Manoeuvre Use the PSL routine:

Position Your position on approach may not change significantly from your normal riding position, but it could be affected by factors such as

- parked vehicles or other obstructions
- other road users
- road markings
- the road surface
- the road width.

Speed Left turns are often sharper than right turns, so reduce speed accordingly.

Look Look out for vehicles stopping just before the junction and pedestrians who may not have seen you. Don't overtake a cyclist or another motorcyclist just before the turn. If you're riding slowly, watch for cyclists coming up on your left – a lifesaver glance over your left shoulder before you turn may be necessary.

Take special care when

- crossing a cycle or bus lane
- pedestrians, especially children, are crossing or waiting to cross
- the road surface is loose or slippery.

When you've completed the turn

- Cancel your signal.
- Check behind, so that you know what's following.
- Adopt the correct road position.
- Accelerate progressively to a speed suitable for the road and traffic conditions, within the set speed limit.

⊕ Emerging

Emerging is when a vehicle leaves one road and joins, crosses or turns into another.

You'll have to judge the speed and distance of any traffic on the road you intend to join or cross, and only emerge when it's safe to do so. This needs care and sometimes patience as well.

You should take care to look for other motorcyclists and cyclists, as their size makes it easy to overlook them. If your view is restricted, they'll be easier to overlook.

When to go

You have to decide when to wait and when it's safe to go. That decision depends largely on your zone of vision.

Your zone of vision is what you can see from your position. It's determined by

- buildings and hedges
- bends in the road or contours in the land
- moving and parked vehicles
- available light and the weather.

As you approach a junction, your zone of vision into the other road usually improves. The last few metres can be critical.

You can only decide whether to wait or go on when you've put yourself in a position where you can see clearly.

Sometimes parked vehicles interfere with your zone of vision, so that you have to creep forward carefully to see more.

If another vehicle or a pedestrian isn't in your zone of vision, you're not usually in theirs.

Looking means that you need to assess the situation, decide whether it's safe and act accordingly.

After you emerge

- Make sure that you cancel your signal.
- Check behind for the speed and position of other traffic.
- Accelerate so that your speed is correct for the road and conditions.
- Keep a safe distance from the vehicle in front.

'Give way' signs or lines

A 'give way' sign and lines across the road mean that you must give way to traffic that's already on the road you intend to enter.

If you can emerge without causing drivers or riders on that road to alter speed or course, you can do so without stopping. Otherwise, you **MUST** stop.

'Stop' signs

You **MUST** always stop at a 'stop' sign, no matter what the traffic situation seems to be on the road you intend to enter. Move off only when you have a clear view and you're sure it's safe.

'Stop' signs are placed at junctions where the visibility is limited. Once you've stopped, you may need to edge forward for a clear view.

Junctions without signs or road markings

Treat these with great care.

Don't assume you have priority at an unmarked junction.

Other traffic

Bends and hills could make it more difficult to see traffic coming towards you.

If a vehicle approaching from your right is signalling to turn left into your road, wait until you're sure that the vehicle is turning, and not pulling up on the left beyond your road, or that the driver has forgotten to cancel their last signal.

Emerging left into a major road

Assess the junction. Check the road signs and markings. Use the OSM/PSL routine.

Observation Look in your mirrors and take rear observation as necessary.

Signal Signal left at the correct time.

Manoeuvre Use the PSL routine:

Position Keep to the left.

Speed Reduce speed – be prepared to stop. Traffic on a minor road must give way to traffic on a major road.

Look Look in all directions at the earliest point from which you can see. Keep looking as you slow down, and stop if necessary.

> **REMEMBER**, an approaching vehicle, particularly a bus or a lorry, can easily mask another moving vehicle that may be overtaking.

You must be aware of pedestrians, cyclists and other motorcyclists who may be alongside. You also need to know how traffic behind is reacting to your manoeuvre.

Emerging right into a major road

Assess the junction. Check road signs and markings. Use the OSM/PSL routine.

Observation Look in your mirrors and take rear observation as necessary.

Signal Signal right in good time.

Manoeuvre Use the PSL routine:

Position Position yourself as close to the centre of the road as is safe.

* In a one-way street, position yourself on the right-hand side of the road.

* When turning right, it's important to take up your position early.

Speed Reduce speed – be prepared to stop. You must give way to traffic on a major road.

Look Look in all directions at the earliest point from which you can see. Keep looking as you slow down, and stop if necessary.

Watch out for

* traffic turning across your path

* pedestrians.

⊙ Types of junction

There are five main types of junction

* T-junctions
* Y-junctions
* staggered junctions
* crossroads
* roundabouts.

Each type of junction can have many variations.

What you intend to do at the junction determines how you approach each type.

T-junctions

This is where a minor road joins a major road.

Normally, the road going straight ahead, along the top of the 'T', has priority.

The minor road may have

- a 'stop' sign and road markings
- a 'give way' sign and road markings
- 'give way' lines only
- no road signs or markings.

If you're riding on the major road

- take note of any road signs and markings
- watch for vehicles turning or emerging, and be aware of the road space required by long vehicles; they may need to use all of the road when turning or emerging
- avoid overtaking on the approach to a T-junction.

If you're riding on the minor road

- take note of the road signs
- look for slippery surfaces or loose chippings
- stop before emerging if your view into the major road is blocked in any way.

Hatch markings
On busier roads, the major road is often split before and after the junction, with a turn-right filter lane protected by white diagonal hatch markings (or chevrons) surrounded by either a broken or unbroken white line.

Join and leave the major road at these junctions exactly as you would a dual carriageway.

Areas of hatch markings are painted on the road

- to separate streams of traffic
- to protect traffic waiting to turn right.

Where the boundary line is solid, don't enter except in an emergency.

Where the boundary line is broken, you shouldn't ride on these markings unless you can see it's safe to do so.

> **REMEMBER**, painted road markings can be slippery, especially when wet.

Junctions on bends

Look well ahead for traffic signs and road markings that indicate priority. These junctions need extra care, especially when turning right from a major road that bends to the left, because

- your field of vision might be limited
- traffic might be approaching quickly from the other direction
- you'll need time to manoeuvre safely.

Your position before you turn mustn't endanger either oncoming traffic or yourself.

Wait until there's a safe gap in the traffic before turning.

Unmarked junctions

Never assume priority over another road if there are no road signs or markings. What's obvious to you might not be obvious to drivers or riders on the other road.

Watch carefully for vehicles

- approaching the junction on the other road
- waiting at the junction
- emerging from the junction to join or cross your path.

Any vehicle crossing

- might assume priority and expect you to give way
- might not assume priority, but might have misjudged your speed or might not have seen you.

Such a vehicle creates a hazard. You should respond in a safe and sensible manner. Anticipate and adjust your speed accordingly to avoid a collision.

Y-junctions

At a Y-junction, the minor road joins the major road at an acute angle. Y-junctions can be deceptive because they often call for little change in direction.

Normally, the road going straight ahead has priority and joining roads have either 'give way' or 'stop' signs. However, there are many exceptions.

Watch out for oncoming vehicles positioned incorrectly. The drivers might have misjudged the junction.

Going straight ahead on the major road

- Look well ahead for road signs and markings.
- Watch out for vehicles emerging to turn left or right.
- Never overtake when approaching any junction.

Emerging from a minor road

If the angle of approach to the major road is very sharp and from the right, the view to your left might be restricted.

If you position your motorcycle towards the major road at a right angle as you approach the 'stop' or 'give way' lines, you'll improve your view.

Staggered junctions

These are junctions where roads join from both the right and the left, but not directly opposite each other, so that the path from one side road to the other is staggered.

If you're riding on the major road, look for

- advance warning signs
- vehicles emerging from either side
- traffic turning into the side roads
- vehicles crossing from one minor road into another.

If you're emerging from either minor road

- Watch for traffic approaching in both directions.
- Watch for traffic emerging from the road opposite.
- Look for slippery surfaces.

If you're crossing from one minor road to another, take extra care. When it's safe to emerge, ride to the centre of the major road opposite the minor road you intend to enter and check the traffic again before entering the minor road.

If you're travelling only a short distance from one minor road to another one almost opposite, make sure the gap in the traffic is wide enough in both directions before emerging. If in doubt, wait.

Crossroads

The procedure when turning at a crossroads is much the same as at any other junction.

You'll need to assess the crossroads as you approach, so look well ahead and check for road signs and markings that might indicate priority.

At crossroads, look for other road users who may not give way.

Riding on the major road

- Watch for road signs and markings.

- Watch for emerging traffic. Be especially careful of vehicles trying to cut across, using gaps in the traffic. They may misjudge your speed or not see you at all.

- Adjust your speed approaching the crossroads.

Turning right

Getting your position and speed correct is vital. Look out for traffic on the road you're joining, as well as on the road you're leaving.

> **REMEMBER**, carry out a lifesaver check before starting to turn, especially if you've had to wait.

Turning right when an oncoming vehicle is also turning right

When two vehicles approaching from opposite directions both want to turn right, there are two methods that can be used. Either method is acceptable, but it will usually be determined by

- the layout of the crossroads

- what course the other driver decides to take

- road markings.

At some crossroads, road markings direct turning nearside to nearside.

Turning offside to offside

The advantage of this method is that both drivers/riders can see oncoming traffic.

In congested traffic conditions, leave a space for approaching traffic to turn right.

Turning nearside to nearside

This method is less safe because the view of oncoming vehicles isn't clear. Watch out for oncoming traffic hidden by larger vehicles and be ready to stop.

Police control or road markings sometimes make this method compulsory.

Defensive riding

Try to make eye contact with the driver of the approaching vehicle to determine which course is best. Your speed should allow you to stop if the other driver cuts across your path.

Approaching on a minor road

If you approach a crossroads on a minor road and want to turn onto the major road, as long as the minor road opposite is clear, you should treat it as if you're emerging from a T-junction.

If you want to turn onto the major road, and another vehicle is approaching the crossroads from the minor road opposite, then

- if you're turning left or going straight on, you should proceed with extra caution and make sure no vehicle from the opposite direction is going to cross your path

- if you're turning right and the other vehicle is going ahead or turning left, you should normally wait for the other vehicle to clear the junction before you make your turn. Otherwise, you'd be cutting across their path

- if you're turning right and the other vehicle is turning right, you should try to make eye contact with the other driver/rider to establish who should proceed, as neither of you has priority.

Unmarked crossroads

Treat unmarked crossroads with extreme caution, since neither road has priority. Never assume you have priority if there are no signs or markings.

Drivers approaching on other roads might also assume they have priority, and an incident could result.

Proceed only when you're sure it's safe to do so.

Remember **LADA** – you must **L**ook, **A**ssess and **D**ecide, before you **A**ct.

Take extra care when your view is restricted by vehicles, walls, hedges or other obstructions.

 Roundabouts

Roundabouts allow traffic from different roads to merge or cross without necessarily stopping.

Priority

Before you enter a roundabout, you normally give way to any traffic approaching from your immediate right. However, you should keep moving if the way is clear.

In a few cases, traffic on the roundabout has to give way to traffic entering. Look out for 'give way' signs and road markings on the roundabout.

Some roundabouts have traffic lights (sometimes part-time) that determine priority.

Always use the OSM/PSL routine on approach.

Approaching a roundabout

Always look well ahead for the advance warning sign, especially at large or complex roundabouts. This will give you a clear picture of the layout of the roundabout, together with route directions.

The sign will enable you to select the most suitable lane in which to approach the roundabout.

Watch out also for advance warnings of appropriate traffic lanes at the roundabout. These are often backed up by road markings, which may include route numbers.

- Get into the correct lane in good time.
- Don't straddle lanes.

- Avoid changing lanes at the last moment.

Where possible, it's a good idea to look across the roundabout and identify the exit you want to take. This will help you to plan the safest course through the roundabout.

Procedure when entering/leaving a roundabout

Adopt the following procedures unless road signs or markings indicate otherwise.

Going left

- Take effective rear observation.
- Indicate left as you approach.
- Approach in the left-hand lane.
- Keep to that lane on the roundabout.
- Maintain a left turn signal through the roundabout.

Using the OSM/PSL routine should ensure that you arrive at a roundabout ready to give way to traffic approaching from the right or keep moving if the way is clear.

Going ahead

- Take effective rear observation.

- No signal is necessary on approach.

- Approach in the left-hand lane. If you can't use the left-hand lane (because, for example, it's blocked), use the lane next to it.

- Keep to the selected lane on the roundabout.

- Take rear observation to the nearside or offside as appropriate.

- Indicate left after you've passed the exit just before the one you intend to take.

- Take a lifesaver glance to the nearside before changing direction if you have to cross a lane on your left to reach your exit.

Going right or full circle

- Take effective rear observation.

- Indicate right as you approach.

- Approach in the right-hand lane.

- Keep to that lane and maintain the signal on the roundabout.

- Take rear observation, especially to the nearside.

- Indicate left after you've passed the exit just before the one you intend to take.

- Take a lifesaver glance to the nearside before changing direction if you have to cross a lane on your left to reach your exit.

REMEMBER, when using the right-hand lane to go ahead, or when turning right, be aware of traffic in the lane to your left.

More than three lanes

Where there are more than three lanes at the approach to the roundabout, use the most appropriate lane on approach and through the roundabout, unless road signs or markings tell you otherwise.

Defensive riding

Always keep an eye on the vehicle in front as you're about to enter the roundabout.

Don't assume that the driver will keep going; they may stop while you're still looking to the right. Many rear-end collisions happen this way. Make sure the vehicle has actually moved away.

Hazards

Roundabouts can be particularly hazardous areas. While negotiating the roundabout, you should be especially aware of

- pedestrians – in many areas, zebra crossings are located near the entrances to and exits from roundabouts. Even if there are no formal crossings, pedestrians may attempt to cross the road at these junctions. Always be aware of pedestrians who may be trying to cross the road

- cyclists and horse riders – they often keep to the outside of the roundabout even when intending to turn right. Take extra care and allow them plenty of room

- long vehicles – because of their length, they might take a different course or straddle lanes as they approach the roundabout and as they go round it. Watch out for their signals and allow for the path the rear of their vehicle follows

- all vehicles – be prepared for vehicles to cross your path to leave at the next exit. Always be on the lookout for their signals

- the road surface – this can become very slippery, particularly when wet. Also, as vehicles travel around roundabouts and bends, fuel can spill onto the road. In wet weather, diesel and oil spillage can be seen as a rainbow-coloured pattern across the road. Even in dry conditions, diesel and oil spillage makes the surface slippery. If you smell diesel, be particularly careful.

Make sure you get into the correct lane in good time for the exit you wish to take.

Mini-roundabouts

Approach these in the same way as a roundabout: slow down and be prepared to give way to traffic from the right. Remember, however, there's less space to manoeuvre and less time to signal. For example, you may not have time to signal left when leaving.

You must pass around the central markings. You should also

- give way to oncoming vehicles turning right
- be sure any vehicle on the roundabout is going to leave it before you join the roundabout
- beware of drivers who are using the roundabout for a U-turn.

Avoid riding over the painted area, since it can be slippery, especially when it's wet.

Double mini-roundabouts

Treat each roundabout separately and give way to traffic from your right. Also, take careful all-round observation before you enter.

Spiral roundabouts

Spiral roundabouts differ from normal roundabouts in that the lanes spiral outwards from the centre of the roundabout and each lane has a designated exit. Road markings are used to keep vehicles in the correct lane, and to guide them towards the appropriate exit.

When you encounter a spiral roundabout

- Make sure you're in the correct lane when approaching and joining the roundabout.
- Follow the road markings for your lane to the relevant exit.
- Beware of drivers who may wish to join your lane from another.

If you need to change lanes, make sure you check it's safe before you do so and signal if necessary.

On a spiral roundabout, following the lanes and road markings will lead you to the appropriate exit.

Multiple roundabouts

At some complex junctions, a large roundabout can incorporate a series of mini-roundabouts at the intersections.

While each mini-roundabout follows the normal rules, with traffic travelling clockwise around them, traffic moving around the central roundabout travels in an anti-clockwise direction. Lanes, signs and road markings give directions, but these are complicated intersections requiring care and concentration.

Look and assess
Keep a good lookout and assess the situation at each mini-roundabout. Look for direction signs and lane markings well in advance.

Junctions on dual carriageways

On a dual carriageway, lanes in one direction are separated from lanes in the other direction by a central reservation. There may be a safety barrier along this central reservation.

Some dual carriageways are very similar to motorways, with slip roads to join and leave. However, motorway regulations don't apply and you may come across slow-moving traffic such as cyclists or farm tractors.

> **REMEMBER**, traffic may be travelling faster than on a single carriageway.

Joining a dual carriageway

Turning left
If there's no slip road, emerge as you would to turn left onto a major road (see the advice earlier in this section).

If there's a slip road

- Use the slip road to adjust your speed to that of traffic on the main carriageway.

- Look for a gap in the traffic and then move into the left-hand lane.

- Remember to take a lifesaver glance just before you move into the left-hand lane.

- Stay in the left-hand lane until you get used to the speed of the traffic in the other lanes.

- Don't emerge unless you're sure you won't cause traffic to alter speed or course.

Turning right

You need to cross the first carriageway before you can join the carriageway you want.

- Assess whether the central reservation is deep enough to protect the full length of your vehicle.

- If the central reservation is deep enough, cross the first carriageway when it's safe and then wait within the central reservation for a gap in the traffic on the second carriageway.

- If the central reservation can't contain the length of your vehicle, you mustn't begin to cross until the dual carriageway is clear in both directions.

- Don't emerge unless you're sure you won't cause traffic on the major road to alter speed or course.

Leaving a dual carriageway

Turning left

If there's no slip road, use the same procedure you would for turning left into a side road.

- Use the OSM/PSL routine and get into the left-hand lane in plenty of time.
- Signal left much earlier than you would on ordinary roads because of the higher speeds involved.
- Reduce your speed in good time.

If there's a slip road on the left, use the same procedure as you would for leaving a motorway (see section 11).

Turning right

The central reservation sometimes has gaps for turning right. Watch out for special approach lanes.

- Use the OSM/PSL routine.
- Signal right and move into the right-hand lane much earlier than you would on normal roads because of the higher speeds involved.
- Observe any lane markings.
- Reduce your speed in good time.
- Don't forget a lifesaver glance before you turn.

Take particular care when turning. You might have to cross the path of fast oncoming traffic in two or more lanes. If in doubt, wait.

> **REMEMBER**, traffic may be travelling at high speeds. If in doubt, wait for a large gap in the traffic.

Section ten
→ Defensive riding

This section covers

- Defensive riding
- Observation
- Hazards
- Lighting conditions
- Other road users

⊕ Defensive riding

The roads today are busier than they've ever been, and they're getting busier all the time. As well as heavy traffic, drivers and riders often have to cope with unpredictable, irrational, offensive and sometimes dangerous driving/riding behaviour. In such conditions, riders need to learn and practise a suitable strategy.

That strategy is called 'defensive riding', sometimes known as 'planned riding'.

Defensive riding is based on effective observation, good anticipation and control. It's about always questioning the actions of other road users and being prepared for the unexpected, so as not to be taken by surprise.

Defensive riding involves

- awareness
- planning
- anticipating
- staying in control

and riding with

- responsibility
- care
- consideration and courtesy.

Are you ready to ride?

Before starting out on any journey, you should consider how you're feeling. Are you fit and well? Are you feeling relaxed or angry and tense? Are you in the right frame of mind to ride?

Have you thought about your clothing? Have you planned your journey? All of these questions need to be addressed before you begin to ride.

Safety

You should put safety above all else. This means having real concern not only for your own safety but also for that of other road users, including the most vulnerable – those walking or cycling.

Expect other people to make mistakes, and be ready to slow down or stop – even if you think you have priority.

Never assume that other road users will follow the rules. They may break them, either deliberately or accidentally. Your safety lies mainly in your own hands. The better your control of your motorcycle and road space, the safer you'll be.

A good example

Your riding should always set a good example to other road users.

Your good example could make a deep impression on someone else, especially a learner or inexperienced road user, and perhaps save lives in the future.

Reducing hostility

With defensive riding, you'll show patience and anticipation. This will help to reduce the number of incidents that result in

- open hostility
- abusive language
- threats
- physical violence.

Avoid the kind of riding that

- gives offence to other road users
- provokes reaction
- creates dangerous situations.

Never ride in a spirit of competition on a public road. Competitive or aggressive riding is the opposite of defensive riding. It increases the risks to everyone.

Make allowances

Make allowances if someone pulls out or cuts in front of you: hold back and increase the distance between you and them. That way, if they brake suddenly, you've given yourself a greater safety margin.

When you check in the mirrors, look and then act sensibly on what you see.

⊕ Observation

Taking effective observation means gathering relevant information on what's going around you, so you're able to make safe decisions.

Look at other road users and assess their

- speed
- driving behaviour
- possible intentions.

At junctions, there's no point in just looking if your view is obstructed by, for example, parked vehicles. You must move carefully into a position where you can see, without moving into the path of passing traffic. Remember LADA

- **L**ook
- **A**ssess and
- **D**ecide before you
- **A**ct.

That's what effective observation is all about.

> **REMEMBER**, fatigue and bad weather can affect your ability to take effective observation.

Observing what's ahead

As a defensive rider, you'll constantly watch and interpret what's happening ahead.

Approaching a bend

Ask yourself

- Can I see the full picture?
- How sharp is the bend?
- Am I in the right position?
- Is my speed right?
- What might I meet?
- Could I stop if I had to?

Approaching a junction

Ask yourself

- Have I seen the whole junction?
- Can others see me?
- Am I sure they've seen me?
- Have I got an escape route if they haven't?

Approaching green traffic lights

Ask yourself

- How long have they been on green?
- Are there many vehicles already waiting at either side of the junction? (If there's a queue, the lights are probably about to change.)
- Do I have time to stop?
- Can the vehicle behind me stop? If it's a large goods vehicle, it might need a greater distance in which to pull up.

Don't

- try to beat the traffic signals by accelerating
- wait until the last moment to brake. Harsh braking can cause skids and loss of control.

Sometimes, drivers anticipate the change of signals and move away while the lights are still showing red and amber. This isn't a safe practice and could result in a collision. Safety cameras are placed at some traffic lights. These record how drivers behave at the lights – including when they move away too soon.

On the open road

When you're riding on the open road, you should be scanning the road ahead, constantly shifting your focus from near to far distance. You should also make frequent mirror checks to keep up to date with the situation behind.

By adopting a systematic approach to observation, you'll be able to identify and prioritise potential hazards in good time.

> **REMEMBER**, always ride at such a speed that you can stop safely within the distance you can see to be clear.

Rear observation

You should always be aware of the position and actions of traffic behind you.

Before you move off, change direction or change speed, you need to know how your action will affect other road users. You must also be aware of traffic likely to overtake.

Timing your rear observation

Look behind before you signal your intention or make any manoeuvre; for example, before

- moving off
- changing direction
- turning right or left
- overtaking
- changing lanes
- slowing or stopping.

For more details, see section 8.

Just looking isn't enough

You must act sensibly on what you see. Take note of the speed, behaviour and possible intentions of traffic behind you.

Another road user's blind spot

Avoid riding in another road user's blind spot for any longer than necessary. This is a particular problem with left-hand-drive lorries, as the driver may not be able to see you and may think it's safe to change lane or overtake.

> **REMEMBER**, a good rider will constantly scan the road ahead and to the side and, through effective rear observation, will be aware of the situation behind.

Zone of vision

Your zone of vision is what you can see as you look forward and to the side from your position. As you approach a junction, your zone of vision into the other road usually improves.

You may need to get very close before you can look far enough into another road to see whether it's safe to proceed. The last few metres are often crucial.

Sometimes, parked vehicles restrict your view so much that you need to stop and creep forward for a proper view before you emerge.

- Look in every direction before you emerge.
- Keep looking as you join the other road.
- Be ready to stop.
- Use all the information available to you; for example, look through the windows of parked vehicles.
- Where your view is restricted, it can help to use the reflections in shop windows to see approaching traffic.

Screen pillar obstruction

Windscreen pillars can cause obstructions to a driver's view of the road. You should be aware that drivers may not have seen you because of this, particularly when they're emerging from junctions.

Other road users

It can be difficult to see some other road users, especially when you're emerging from a junction. Those who are particularly at risk are

- pedestrians – they frequently cross at junctions and may find it difficult to judge the speed and course of approaching traffic
- cyclists – they can be difficult to see, as they may be obscured by trees and other objects, especially if they're riding close to the side of the road. They might be approaching faster than you expect
- other motorcyclists – like cyclists, they're often less easy to see than other traffic, but they're likely to be moving much faster than cyclists.

If another vehicle or a pedestrian isn't in your zone of vision, you're not usually in theirs.

Making eye contact with other road users helps you to know whether they've seen you.

> **REMEMBER**, never rely solely on a quick glance – give yourself time to take in the whole scene.

Being seen

Many accidents or near misses occur at junctions, when a vehicle emerges into the path of an oncoming motorcyclist and the driver claims 'I just didn't see you.'

This can be the result of 'motion camouflage' or 'looming': an optical effect that causes the motorcycle to 'disappear' into the background before 'reappearing' close to the junction, often after the driver has started to emerge.

As you approach a junction where you can see a vehicle waiting to emerge, ask yourself

- Has the driver seen me?
- What if I haven't been seen?
- Would it help to sound the horn?

Small changes to your road position on the approach to a junction can break the looming effect and help drivers see you earlier.

Using dipped headlights in the daytime and wearing bright clothing also increase your chances of being seen.

⊕ Hazards

A hazard is any situation that could require you to adjust your speed or change course. To identify a hazard, you must look well ahead for clues such as

- road signs
- changes in road conditions
- parked vehicles
- junctions
- other road users.

Effective observation and anticipation enable you to see the clues and respond safely.

As soon as you've recognised a hazard, you must assess

- how to deal with it safely
- how your actions will affect other road users.

Recognising hazards

Recognising, prioritising and responding correctly to hazards are skills that develop with experience. It's important to allow enough time and space to see and respond to a hazard before it develops into real danger.

To say that you have to see the hazard may sound obvious but it requires you to be looking in the right place.

Once you've identified a hazard, you'll need to take some form of action. This action will vary from one hazard to another.

Any action that involves a change of speed or course is called a manoeuvre. A manoeuvre can vary from slowing slightly to turning on a very busy road.

The defensive rider is always

- in the correct position
- travelling at the correct speed for the road, traffic and weather conditions
- in the right gear
- anticipating and prepared for the next change in the traffic situation.

Positioning yourself too late can be dangerous. Ask yourself

- Can I see and be seen?
- Are other vehicles restricting my course of action?
- Have I enough room to get out of any difficulties?

Approaching any hazard

Follow the OSM/PSL routine every time you recognise a hazard.

Observation Check the position of following traffic using your mirrors or by looking behind at an appropriate time.

Signal If necessary, signal your intention to change course or slow down. Signal clearly and in good time.

Manoeuvre Carry out the manoeuvre if it's still safe to do so. Manoeuvre has three phases: Position, Speed and Look.

Position Get into the correct position in good time to negotiate the hazard. This helps other road users to anticipate what you intend to do.

Avoid cutting in front of other riders or drivers. If lanes are closed or narrow because of roadworks, move into the correct lane in good time.

Speed Ask yourself

- Could I stop in time if the vehicle in front braked suddenly?
- Am I going too fast for the road conditions?
- Am I in the right gear to keep control?

Slow down as you approach a hazard. Always be ready to stop.

Look Keep looking ahead to assess all possible dangers. This is particularly important at a junction. Look in all directions, even if you aren't turning.

If you're joining a road, keep looking as you turn from one road to the other. Watch out for

- traffic turning across your path
- pedestrians.

Allowing time and space

Always leave yourself enough time and space to cope with what's ahead.

- Scan the road ahead, in the far and near distance – especially in town, where things change quickly.
- Check the traffic behind you regularly.
- Watch for clues about what's likely to happen next.

For example, a parked car is a potential hazard if the driver is sitting in it, or you see vapour from the exhaust in cold weather. This could indicate that

- a door might open suddenly
- the car might pull out without warning.

If you can see underneath a parked vehicle and notice someone's feet at the other side, remember that the pedestrian might not be able to see you and could step into the road. Children can be particularly difficult to see and may run out without looking.

Separation distances

Always keep a good separation distance between you and the vehicle in front. Leave a gap of at least one metre or yard for each mph of your speed, or use the two-second rule (see section 8).

In bad conditions, leave at least double the distance or a four-second time gap.

Tailgating
When a vehicle behind is too close to you, ease off the throttle very gradually and increase the gap between you and the vehicle in front. This will give you a greater safety margin. If another road user pulls into the space in front of you, drop back until you've restored your safety margin.

Large vehicles
Take extra care when following large vehicles, especially at roundabouts, junctions and entrances. The driver might have to take a course that seems incorrect to you; for example, moving out to the right before turning left.

Keep well back from any large vehicles that are in the process of manoeuvring to the left or right. Be patient and don't try to pass while they're manoeuvring.

Large vehicles can also block your view. Your ability to see and plan ahead will be improved if you keep back.

> **REMEMBER**, if you're following a large vehicle too closely, the driver might not be able to see you in their mirrors. If you can't see their mirrors, the driver can't see you.

Country roads

These roads present their own hazards. Take extra care and reduce your speed as you approach bends and junctions.

If you're riding a slow-moving scooter or small motorcycle on a narrow road, a queue of traffic may build up behind you. Look for a safe place to pull in and let the faster traffic go past. This should prevent drivers from becoming impatient and attempting to overtake dangerously.

Bends and junctions
Bends can often be sharper than you think they're going to be. They may also obscure other, more vulnerable road users, such as pedestrians, horse riders and cyclists, or larger slow-moving farm vehicles, which may take up the whole width of the road.

Junctions, especially minor junctions or entrances to farm premises, aren't always signed and may be partially hidden.

Road surfaces

On country roads, be prepared to find

- worn road surfaces
- mud
- hedge cuttings
- leaves in the autumn.

If you see mud or hedge cuttings on the road, anticipate finding the cause around the next bend. This may be farm machinery or farm animals. Either way, it will be a slow-moving hazard and you need to be prepared to stop.

Other road users

Many roads in country areas have no pavements or footpaths. Where this is the case, pedestrians are advised to walk on the right-hand side of the road so they can see oncoming traffic. You should always be prepared to find people walking or jogging on your side of the road.

Horse riders and cyclists are also found often on country roads. Give them plenty of space, always be patient and wait until it's safe before overtaking, especially on narrow or winding roads.

Narrow roads with passing places

On single-track roads, look well ahead and be prepared to stop. If you see an oncoming vehicle

- pull into the passing place if it's on the left
- be prepared to reverse into a passing place if necessary
- wait opposite a passing place on the right.

If a driver wishes to overtake, pull into or stop opposite a passing place to allow them to do so.

⊕ Lighting conditions

In the dark, seeing hazards is more difficult. The clues are there, but you have to pick them out. Look for

- illuminated or reflective road signs
- reflectors between white lines
- the glow of vehicle headlights on buildings, trees and hedges, indicating bends and junctions.

In the dark

- It can be difficult to judge distance and speed from the headlights of approaching vehicles.
- The bright lights on some vehicles make it difficult to see pedestrians, cyclists and any vehicle with dim lights.
- Keep a good lookout for pedestrian crossings, traffic lights and other road users, and don't let shop and advertising lights distract you.

More information about riding at night can be found in section 13.

Wet roads

The reflections from wet surfaces make it more difficult to see unlit objects and can be distracting.

The combination of rain and darkness further reduces visibility. Keep your speed down on unlit or poorly lit roads. Remember, your stopping distance increases in the wet.

Unlit side view

When you're sideways on to other road users, you'll be less easily seen; for example, when passing side turnings or emerging right or left.

Wearing reflective material will help other road users to see you.

⊕ Other road users

Remember that you're not the only person using the road. It's your responsibility to be aware of other road users and to show them consideration.

Cyclists

Make allowances for cyclists. They have every right to be on the road, but they're vulnerable. The younger the cyclist, the more vulnerable they're likely to be.

Allow cyclists plenty of room; they might

- glance round, showing they could be about to move out or turn
- veer suddenly into your path
- be carrying items that may affect their control and balance
- weave about, slow down, or stop on uphill gradients
- swerve around potholes or drain covers or to avoid being hit by carelessly opened vehicle doors
- have problems in bad weather, particularly when there are strong side winds
- have difficulty on poor road surfaces or where tramlines are set into the road.

Look out for them particularly when you're

- in slow-moving traffic
- emerging from a junction
- negotiating a roundabout.

They could be travelling faster than you first think, so never rely solely on a quick glance.

Don't assume that cyclists will always adopt a position on the left of the road or use cycle lanes; it's sometimes safer for them to adopt a more central position in the road. Don't ride aggressively or try to intimidate them.

When travelling at low speeds, such as at junctions, cyclists are likely to be more unstable and therefore more vulnerable. Give them plenty of room.

Learner drivers and riders

Learners might take longer to react in traffic situations, or may make mistakes. If this happens, keep calm and be patient. Allow extra room for safety, in case the learner stops or manoeuvres suddenly.

Powered vehicles used by disabled people

These small vehicles (also known as invalid carriages) can be used on the pavement and on the road. They're extremely vulnerable when they're on the road because of

- their small size
- their low speed – they have a maximum speed of 8 mph (12 km/h).

Their small size means they aren't easy to see. On a dual carriageway where the speed limit exceeds 50 mph (80 km/h) they should be displaying an amber flashing light, but on other roads you may not have that advance warning.

Buses and coaches

Look well ahead when you see buses and coaches at a bus stop. Be aware of

- people getting off the bus or coach. They may not look properly before they cross the road – and even if they do look, their view is often restricted
- buses and coaches pulling away from the bus stop. If they're signalling to move out, give way to them if you can do so safely.

Pedestrians

Always ride carefully and slowly in areas where there are likely to be pedestrians, such as residential areas and town centres.

Be particularly careful in Home Zones and Quiet Lanes, where people could be using the whole of the road for a range of activities.

Always look out for pedestrians when

- turning from one road into another – give way to people who are crossing the road into which you're turning
- approaching pedestrian crossings. Never overtake on the approach to a crossing
- riding past a bus or tram stop, as pedestrians may walk out into the road.

Older people
Several factors make older people more vulnerable.

If they have poor eyesight or hearing, they might not be aware of approaching traffic. They might not be able to judge the speed of approaching traffic when crossing the road. Even when they do realise the danger, they may be unable to move quickly, or they may become flustered.

They may also take longer to cross the road. Be patient and don't hurry them by revving your engine or edging forwards.

People with disabilities
Take special care around people with disabilities.

Visually impaired people may not be able to see you approaching. They may carry a white cane or use a guide dog. The guide dog has a distinctive loop-type harness. Remember, the dog is trained to wait if there's a vehicle nearby.

A person with hearing difficulties isn't easy to identify, so take extra care if a pedestrian fails to look your way as you approach. Remember they may not be aware of your presence. They may have a guide dog wearing a distinctive yellow or burgundy coat.

Those who are deaf and blind may carry a white cane with a red band or may be using a guide dog with a red-and-white harness. They may not see or hear instructions or signals.

> **REMEMBER**, always think of the other road user, not just of yourself.

Children
Take extra care where children might be around, particularly in residential areas and near schools and parks.

Ride carefully and slowly past schools, especially at school start and finish times. Be aware that

- a school crossing patrol may stop you to escort children across the road
- children may be getting on or off a bus showing a 'school bus' sign.

Children are impulsive and unpredictable. Therefore, ride slowly in narrow roads where parked cars obscure your view.

Look out for parked ice-cream vans. Children are usually more interested in ice cream than they are in traffic and they may forget to look before running across the road.

Animals

Animals are easily frightened by noise and vehicles coming close to them. You should

- ride slowly and quietly; don't sound the horn
- keep your engine speed low; don't rev your engine or accelerate rapidly once you've passed them

- always watch out for animals on unfenced roads, as they may step out in front of you. You should always be able to stop safely within the distance you can see to be clear, especially at night when your lights are dipped.

Give animals as much room as possible.

People in charge of animals

If someone in charge of animals signals to you to stop, do so and switch off your engine.

Horses

Be particularly careful when approaching horses, especially those being ridden by children.

As a motorcyclist, you should

- look out for horses being led or ridden on the road
- take extra care and keep your speed down at left-hand bends, especially on narrow country roads
- slow down when you see a horse rider on the road.

Be aware that at roundabouts and at junctions where a horse rider is turning right, they may signal right but keep to the left-hand side of the road (and the outside lane round the roundabout) for safety.

As you approach a horse rider from behind

- Slow down, give them plenty of room and be prepared to stop.
- Don't sound your horn or rev your engine. Horses can be easily scared by noise and may panic around fast-moving vehicles.
- Look out for signals given by the riders and heed a request to slow down or stop.

Always pass horses slowly, giving them plenty of room.

Take special care when meeting what appears to be a riding-school group. Many of the riders might be inexperienced and some may be on leading reins. A good indication of this is if there's an adult walking alongside a horse and rider.

Also look out for horse-drawn vehicles and treat them in a similar way to horses being ridden.

Wild animals

Over 2 million deer live wild in Great Britain. Increases in the deer population, combined with a rise in traffic volumes, have resulted in a large number of road traffic incidents involving deer each year.

Incidents happen throughout the year, but they're more likely during May, and from October through to January. The risks increase around dawn and dusk, when deer activity peaks, coinciding with rush hours.

To minimise the risk of collisions with deer

- Pay attention to deer warning signs.
- Keep your speed down.
- Take extra care at dawn and dusk, when deer activity is at its highest.
- Use your headlights on main beam if there's no traffic, so you can see any deer. Dip them if you see a deer, otherwise it may freeze in your path.
- Be aware that many deer could be in the area – not just the ones you spot.

Report any collisions with deer to the police non-emergency number, 101, so that a deer warden can attend. If the animal is dead, then you should report it to the local authority so they can remove it.

Section eleven
⊙ Riding on motorways

This section covers

- Riding on motorways
- Motorway signs and signals
- Joining a motorway
- On the motorway
- Lane discipline
- Smart motorways
- Overtaking

- Leaving a motorway
- Weather conditions
- Stopping on motorways
- Motorways at night
- Roadworks
- Traffic officers

⊙ Riding on motorways

Motorways differ from ordinary roads in that they're designed to help traffic travel faster and in greater safety.

Motorways are statistically safer than other roads in relation to the number of incidents occurring. However, when they do happen, motorway incidents usually occur at higher speed and involve more vehicles. As a result, injuries are usually more serious – and are more likely to result in loss of life.

Because of the higher speeds, it's important that you can be seen easily by other road users. Wear high-visibility clothing and ride with your headlights on dipped beam.

You'll find that you're exposed to wind turbulence, particularly from larger vehicles. You'll need to anticipate the effect so that you can keep full control of your machine.

REMEMBER, because traffic travels faster on motorways, conditions change more rapidly. Use the two-second rule and look well ahead. Don't just focus on the vehicle in front.

Before you ride on a motorway

- You must hold a full licence for the category of motorcycle you're riding. Riders who are moving up to larger motorcycles are classed as learners on the larger machines and **MUST NOT** ride them on motorways until the appropriate practical test has been passed.
- You should have a thorough knowledge of all rules within The Highway Code, but particularly those dealing with motorways.
- You need to know and understand motorway warning signs and signals.

REMEMBER, motorcycles under 50 cc **MUST NOT** be used on motorways.

Concentration

You need to be fit and alert to ride anywhere, but particularly so on motorways. Never use the motorway if you feel tired or unwell.

General guidelines on dealing with fatigue are given in section 1 but the problems when riding on motorways tend to be greater because of the long distances involved and the monotony of the journey.

Research has found that fatigue accounts for 15–20% of incidents on monotonous roads (especially motorways). If your journey seems boring and you feel drowsy, take a break at the first opportunity: either stop at the next service area or leave the motorway and find a safe place to rest and recover. Plan plenty of rest stops, especially at night.

Parking is forbidden except at service areas. If you need rest, you'll sometimes have to travel a long distance before an exit or a service area. Remember it's an offence to stop on the hard shoulder, an exit road or a slip road, except in an emergency.

Check your motorcycle

High speeds and long distances increase the risk of mechanical failure. You should carry out the following checks on your motorcycle before using a motorway.

- **Tyres** They must be in good condition and inflated to the correct pressure. Follow the guidance given in the vehicle handbook, which may state different pressures to be used when carrying a passenger or load.
- **Brakes** Check they can stop you safely.
- **Steering** Check it's in good order.
- **Instruments and warning lights** Make sure they're all working correctly.
- **Mirrors** (if fitted) Make sure they're clean and correctly positioned.
- **Lights and indicators** Make sure they're all working correctly.

For safety, convenience and good vehicle care, you should also check the following items.

- **Fuel** Make sure you have enough fuel to avoid running out between service areas.
- **Oil** High speeds may mean your engine uses oil faster. Running out can be dangerous and costly.
- **Water** (liquid-cooled engines) Higher speeds can mean a warmer engine, especially in traffic tailbacks in hot weather.

Make sure any load is secure
Check that everything carried on your motorcycle or trailer is safe and secure.

If anything should fall from your motorcycle or from another vehicle, stop on the hard shoulder and use the emergency telephone to inform the authorities. **Never** try to retrieve it yourself.

A quick check before using the motorway might prevent a breakdown during your journey.

⊕ Motorway signs and signals

Motorway signs

Leading to the motorway

Direction signs from ordinary roads to the motorway have white lettering and figures on a blue panel, often bordered in white.

These signs may stand alone or be included in other, larger signs of various colours.

On the motorway

You may find the following types of sign on the motorway

- advance direction signs

- countdown markers

- signs giving information about service areas

- signs with a brown background. These indicate tourist attractions that can be reached by leaving at the next exit.

All these signs are very much larger than those on ordinary roads because you need to be able to see them from a distance. This is a good reminder that you must leave more room for all manoeuvres when riding on a motorway.

Each junction has an identifying number, which corresponds with current road maps. This is to help you plan your route and know where you need to leave the motorway.

Speed-limit signs

- Signs that display a speed within a red ring indicate a mandatory speed limit. These are often seen at roadworks or on overhead gantries. You **MUST** obey the signs. If you don't, you risk prosecution.

- Black-and-white rectangular signs show recommended maximum speeds.

Motorway signals

Signals warn of dangers ahead, such as

- incidents
- fog
- icy roads
- delays
- standing traffic.

Flashing amber lights

Look out for flashing amber lights and signs, either on the central reservation or overhead. These warn you of

- lane closures
- roadworks
- other hazards.

They might also show a temporary speed limit. You should

- slow down to the speed limit
- be ready to slow down even further to pass the obstacle or danger
- look out for signs giving further advice
- don't speed up until you see the sign ending the temporary restriction (or there are no more flashing amber lights).

Red lights

Some signs have flashing red lights as well.

A red light (it may be a red 'X') warns you that you **MUST NOT** go beyond the red light in that lane. You should

- start to slow down in good time
- be ready to change lanes.

If the red light flashes on a slip road, you **MUST NOT** enter that slip road.

If a red light flashes on the central reservation or at the side of the road, you **MUST NOT** go beyond the signal in any lane.

⊙ Joining a motorway

You can join a motorway

- where a main road becomes a motorway. This is indicated by a specially worded sign
- by joining at any entry point. A slip road leads onto the motorway.

At an entry point where a slip road leads to the motorway, adjust your speed to that of the traffic already on the motorway before joining it. Give priority to traffic already on the motorway.

Join where there's a suitable gap in the left-hand lane. Use the Observation – Signal – Manoeuvre/ Position – Speed – Look (OSM/PSL) routine. A lifesaver glance will verify the position of other vehicles. Try to avoid stopping at the end of the slip road unless queuing to join other slow-moving traffic.

A tapering chevron helps you to gauge the distance to where the slip road joins the motorway.

At some slip roads there's no need to join by merging because the joining lane may continue as a dedicated lane. Signs and road markings normally indicate this arrangement.

Do

- indicate your intention to join the motorway
- make sure you can be seen
- assess the speed of the traffic on the motorway before you try to join.

Don't

- ride across the chevrons, except in an emergency
- force your way into the traffic stream
- ride along the hard shoulder.

Once you've joined the motorway, keep in the left-hand lane until you've had time to judge and adjust to the speed of the traffic already on the motorway.

In some cases, the lane merges from the right. Take extra care when joining or meeting traffic at these locations.

⊕ On the motorway

Effective observation

Keep your eyes moving between the road ahead and your mirrors, so that you always know what's happening all around you.

Continually reassess the movement of the vehicles

- directly ahead (in the near and far distance)
- alongside you
- behind you.

At high speeds, situations change rapidly. Effective observation helps you prepare for any sudden developments.

For example, an increase in the number of vehicles ahead could mean that traffic is slowing down and 'bunching'.

If you see serious congestion ahead, you can use your hazard warning lights (if fitted) briefly to alert drivers behind you. This can reduce the risk of rear-end collisions, especially in bad weather.

Keeping your distance

The faster the traffic, the more time and space you need.

You must give yourself greater margins than on ordinary roads and make sure there's enough space between you and the vehicle ahead.

Traffic normally travels faster on motorways because there are usually no

- ordinary junctions
- sharp bends
- roundabouts
- steep hills
- traffic lights.

Slow-moving vehicles are generally forbidden.

Note: some motorway links, where motorway regulations also apply, do have roundabouts and sharp bends.

How big a gap?
Leave a gap of at least one metre or yard for each mph of your speed. A useful method of judging this is to use the two-second rule (see section 8).

This rule is reinforced on some motorways where there are chevrons painted on the carriageway. Keep at least two chevrons between you and the vehicle in front.

Bad weather
Leave at least double the space if the road is wet.

In icy conditions, you'll need up to 10 times the stopping distance that you need in dry conditions.

Obstructions

If vehicles ahead switch on their hazard warning lights, be prepared for slow-moving or stationary traffic.

Look well ahead and leave yourself plenty of room. Check behind to see how the traffic behind you is reacting.

If you find yourself catching up with slower-moving traffic, there could be an obstruction ahead. Be aware that other vehicles may be slowing gradually to avoid the need to brake. You won't have any warning from their brake lights in these situations.

⊕ Lane discipline

Lane discipline is vitally important on motorways. You should normally ride in the left-hand lane.

- Don't change lanes unless you need to.
- Ride in the centre of the lane.
- Don't wander into another lane.

Two-lane motorways

On a two-lane motorway, the correct position for normal riding is in the left-hand lane.

The right-hand (offside) lane is for overtaking only. Once you've overtaken, you should return to the left-hand lane as soon as it's safe to do so. It isn't the 'fast lane'.

Large goods vehicles are permitted to use either lane. They're subject to the same rules on lane use described above.

Motorways with three or more lanes

Because of the volume of traffic on three-lane motorways, many are being widened to four or more lanes in each direction.

Keep to the left-hand lane unless there are slower vehicles ahead – it's possible to stay in the centre or outer lanes while you're overtaking a number of slower moving vehicles, but don't stay in these lanes

- longer than you have to
- if you're delaying traffic behind you.

Drivers of large goods vehicles, buses, coaches or any vehicle towing a trailer aren't allowed to use the extreme right-hand lane of a motorway with more than two lanes, unless one or more lanes are temporarily closed.

Don't stay in an overtaking lane longer than it takes you to move out, overtake and move in again safely. Make sure you don't block traffic that isn't allowed to use the outer lane.

Changing lanes

Don't change lanes unnecessarily. You should

* keep your vehicle steady in the centre of the lane
* not wander into another lane.

OSM/PSL routine

Always use the OSM/PSL routine well before you intend to change lanes. At higher speeds, you must start the routine much earlier.

Look and, if necessary, signal in good time. Remember, vehicles might come up behind you very quickly.

The sooner you indicate, the sooner other road users are warned of your intended movement. They'll expect a change in the traffic pattern and have time to prepare for it.

Crawler and climbing lanes

A steep hill on a motorway might have a crawler or climbing lane to avoid heavy vehicles slowing down the flow of traffic.

When other vehicles join

After you pass an exit, there's usually an entrance where other vehicles can join the motorway.

- Don't try to race them while they're on the slip road.
- Look well ahead; if there are several vehicles joining the motorway, be prepared to adjust your speed.
- Show consideration for traffic joining the motorway and, if it's safe, move to another lane to make it easier for joining traffic to merge.
- Take extra care if the motorway curves, as drivers on the slip road may have difficulty seeing vehicles on the motorway.

Motorway interchanges

Where motorways merge or separate, you might be required to change lanes, sometimes more than once.

Pay attention to the overhead direction signs and move into the correct lane in good time.

Where the hatch markings indicate splitter islands, stay in your lane.

Assess conditions well ahead and watch for other drivers changing lanes.

Changes in traffic conditions

Traffic conditions can vary as much on a motorway as on an ordinary road.

There can be rush-hour traffic near cities, heavy traffic near roadworks and constantly busy sections in other places.

⊙ Smart motorways

On some sections of motorway, technology is in place to reduce congestion and improve your journey times. These roads are known as 'smart motorways'. The technology is also referred to as active traffic management (ATM).

Smart motorways use traffic management technology to vary speed limits as traffic volume increases. Riders may also be allowed to use the hard shoulder as an extra lane during busy periods.

Types of smart motorway

Controlled motorway

Controlled motorways have three or more lanes, with variable speed limits shown on overhead signs. These speed limits are shown inside a red circle and are legally enforceable. The hard shoulder on controlled motorways should only be used in an emergency.

All-lane running

On a smart motorway converted to all-lane running, the hard shoulder is permanently used as an extra lane. Refuge areas with emergency telephones are provided at least every 2500 metres, in case of an emergency or breakdown, and riders receive regular information updates via overhead signs. The signs display information on the current mandatory variable speed limits, as well as indicating whether lanes are closed.

Dynamic hard shoulder

Sections of smart motorway with a dynamic hard shoulder use the hard shoulder to provide extra capacity during busy periods. The hard shoulder is marked with a solid white line and riders/drivers are only allowed to use it as a running lane when the overhead signs say it's available. If the sign above the hard shoulder displays a red X or is blank, you must only enter it in an emergency.

Riding on a smart motorway

- Overhead signs display speed limits to manage traffic and give information about incidents or driving conditions. They also tell you which lanes are available for you to use. Obey the signs; they're there to keep the traffic moving.

- Red crosses are used to show when lanes, including the hard shoulder, shouldn't be used. When you see a red X above a lane, don't ride in that lane.

- If a speed limit is displayed directly above the hard shoulder, you can ride on it. If you see a red X or no speed limit displayed above the hard shoulder, you should only use it in an emergency or breakdown.

What to do in a breakdown

If you have a problem with your vehicle when you're riding on a smart motorway, you should try to leave at the next exit or pull into a motorway service area. If you can't leave the motorway, then you should stop in one of the emergency refuge areas, where you'll be able to call for help using the roadside telephone.

If it isn't possible to do any of these things, try to get your motorcycle off the carriageway and onto the verge or hard shoulder – if one is available.

You should

- switch on your hazard warning lights (if fitted) so that you can be seen more easily by other road users and anyone coming out to help

- dismount to the left-hand side and wait behind the barrier if you're able to do so.

By making a few simple checks, like making sure you have enough fuel, checking and replacing worn or damaged tyres, and servicing your vehicle regularly, you can greatly reduce the chances of breaking down during your journey.

For more information on smart motorways, visit this website.

www.gov.uk/government/collections/smart-motorways

⊕ Overtaking

Leave a safe distance between you and the vehicle you intend to overtake.

Use the appropriate parts of the OSM/PSL routine. For example

Observation Check behind to verify the speed, course and position of traffic behind you.

Position Position yourself so that you can see well past the vehicle in front.

Speed Make sure you're going fast enough or can accelerate quickly enough to overtake without blocking any vehicle coming up behind.

Look Look ahead and behind to check whether there's anything preventing you from overtaking safely; for example, a lane closure ahead or traffic coming up much faster from behind in the right-hand lane.

Try to anticipate whether the vehicle ahead will move out to overtake.

Remember LADA

- **L**ook
- **A**ssess well ahead
- **D**ecide – don't rush
- **A**ct – only when you're sure it's safe.

Observation

Remember that vehicles coming up in the right-hand lane are likely to be moving faster than you are. Watch for vehicles returning to the lane you intend to use.

Signal

You must signal well before you start to move out. This gives drivers behind you plenty of time to anticipate what you intend to do and could influence any manoeuvres they're planning.

Pulling out

Take a lifesaver glance into the blind spot before moving out smoothly into an overtaking lane. Cancel your signal and overtake as quickly and safely as possible.

As you overtake a large goods vehicle, bus or coach, expect to be buffeted by the changing air pressure. Don't ride too close to the vehicle you're overtaking.

Moving back to the left

Pass the vehicle and signal, if necessary, before moving back to the left as soon as you're sure it's safe to do so. Don't cut in too soon in front of the vehicle you've just passed.

Look well ahead for any vehicles about to move into the lane that you intend to join. Allow plenty of room. Finally, make sure your indicator signal cancels properly.

Overtaking on the left

Never overtake on the left unless the traffic is moving in queues and the queue on your right is moving more slowly than the one you're in.

Overtaking on busy motorways

If you come up behind traffic moving more slowly than you are when you're overtaking, be patient and don't

- intimidate the driver ahead by flashing your headlights or riding dangerously close behind
- filter between fast-moving lanes of traffic.

Defensive riding

Let faster traffic pass you. If other road users are breaking the speed limit, don't add to the danger by trying to enforce the legal speed limit.

Don't move to a lane on the left to overtake.

Never use the hard shoulder to overtake – unless directed to do so by traffic signs at roadworks, by police officers or by traffic officers in uniform.

Ride defensively and let faster traffic pass you. Don't move to a lane on the left to overtake.

⊕ Leaving a motorway

Unless you're going to the end of the motorway, you'll leave by moving left from the left-hand lane into a slip road. Position yourself in the left-hand lane in plenty of time.

Plan well ahead, particularly on motorways with three or more lanes.

Road signs

Use the road signs and markers to help you time your exit and use your mirrors and indicators appropriately. You'll have plenty of time to observe the signs and markers, so there's no need to rush.

One mile before the exit
There'll be a junction sign with road numbers, unless there are exits very close together.

Half a mile before the exit
You'll see a sign with the names of places you can reach from that exit.

Countdown markers
These are positioned at 270 metres (300 yards), 180 metres (200 yards) and 90 metres (100 yards) before the start of the slip road.

Where a lane splits off from the motorway as a dedicated lane, countdown markers aren't provided.

To leave the motorway

Use your mirrors and signal in good time. Remember to use the OSM/PSL routine.

Get into the left-hand lane early. On a motorway with three or more lanes, this could mean changing lanes more than once. You must follow the OSM/PSL routine for each change of lane.

> **REMEMBER**, use your mirrors and signal left in good time to move into the left-hand lane.

Don't

* move to the left more than one lane at a time
* cut straight across into the slip road at the last moment.

The hard shoulder is **not** an exit road, and you must avoid queuing on it.

Occasionally, where motorways merge, there may be an exit just before the one you intend to take. In these cases, or where there are service areas near to exits, look well ahead for the direction signs to ensure you take the right exit.

If you miss your exit, carry on to the next one.

Speed when leaving a motorway

After riding at motorway speeds for some time, your judgement of speed will almost certainly be affected: 40 or 45 mph (64 or 72 km/h) will seem more like 20 mph (32 km/h). Stay aware of your speed.

* Adjust your riding to suit the new conditions.
* Check your speedometer. It will give you the accurate speed.

Remember, even if you don't have to reduce your speed because the road you're joining is a dual carriageway, drivers of some other vehicles have to obey a lower speed limit. Be aware that they may reduce their speed.

Reduce speed at first

For the sake of safety, reduce your speed until you're used to the change of conditions. It could take you time to adjust.

Motorway slip roads and link roads often have sharp curves, which should be taken at much lower speeds. The road surface on these curves may be slippery. Take care and look out for spilt diesel fuel.

Look ahead for traffic queuing at a roundabout or traffic signals.

When you leave the motorway, it could take you time to adjust to lower speed limits.

End of motorway

There will be an 'end of motorway' sign wherever you leave the motorway network. This means that the road you're joining has different rules.

Remember to watch for any signs telling you what these are, particularly

- speed limits
- a dual carriageway
- two-way traffic
- a clearway
- a motorway link road
- part-time traffic lights.

> **REMEMBER**, because of the change in traffic conditions, you need to watch for pedestrians, cyclists and other road users who are prohibited on motorways.

⊕ Weather conditions

The advice given in section 12 is even more important on a motorway.

Wet weather

In heavy rain, the surface spray from other vehicles, especially large ones, will seriously reduce visibility, as well as increasing your stopping distance. Make sure that you

- make yourself visible. Use dipped headlights and wear bright clothing
- can see clearly. Keep your visor or goggles clean
- adjust your speed to suit the conditions and leave larger separation distances – at least double the normal gap.

Ice or frost

Ice or frost on the road can seriously affect your motorcycle's handling. Try to avoid riding in these conditions; consider an alternative form of transport.

Try to anticipate the road surface conditions. If your steering feels light, it's an indication that there may be frost or ice. Be very gentle with your use of the controls.

Allow up to 10 times the normal distance for braking.

Side winds

A sudden gust of wind can blow you off course. Keep your speed down where there's a danger of side winds.

Riding more slowly will help you to keep control. You need to be especially careful as you emerge from the shelter of a large vehicle when overtaking or being overtaken, especially on exposed stretches of road.

In severe windy weather, some exposed stretches of motorway are closed for safety reasons. Check with a local radio station or motoring organisation before setting out.

> **REMEMBER**, in strong winds, drivers of high-sided vehicles or those towing caravans are likely to experience difficulties. Allow for this when riding near these vehicles.

Fog

Riding on the motorway when the weather is foggy can be particularly hazardous.

If there's fog on the motorway, you must be able to stop well within the distance you can see to be clear.

- Use dipped headlights.
- Make sure that your visor or goggles are clean and aren't hindering your view ahead.
- Wear bright clothing. This will help other drivers to see you.

Fog can drift quickly and is often patchy.

If a motorway warning sign shows 'FOG'

- Be prepared.
- Reduce your speed in good time.

Multiple pile-ups can happen in foggy conditions. They're usually caused by drivers who are

- travelling too fast
- driving too close to the vehicle in front
- assuming there's nothing in the fog ahead.

If there's fog

- Switch on your fog lights (if fitted) if visibility falls below 100 metres (328 feet).
- Be prepared to leave the motorway.
- Be on the alert for incidents ahead.
- Watch out for emergency vehicles coming up behind, possibly on the hard shoulder.

> **REMEMBER**, don't 'hang on' to the lights of the vehicle ahead. You'll be too close to brake if it stops suddenly.

⊕ Stopping on motorways

You must only stop on a motorway if

- red lights or other signs or signals tell you to do so
- you're asked to stop by the police, traffic officers or Driver and Vehicle Standards Agency (DVSA) officers
- it's an emergency
- it will prevent an incident.

Motorway service areas have lane markings and signs to help direct you.

If you need to stop for a rest, find a service area. The hard shoulder isn't for parking or resting.

Breakdowns

If your motorcycle breaks down, try to get onto the hard shoulder. When you've stopped

- park as far to the left as you can, away from the traffic
- switch on your hazard warning lights (if fitted)
- switch on your parking lights in poor visibility or at night
- make your way to the nearest emergency telephone and call for assistance. Never attempt even minor repairs.

Disabled riders

Disabled riders may be less able to manually manoeuvre a heavy motorcycle, motorcycle/sidecar combination or trike, even for a short distance, in the event of a vehicle breakdown.

Some breakdown/recovery schemes offer a priority response system for people who are registered with them as being disabled. If your disabilities are likely to leave you in a vulnerable position in the event of a vehicle breakdown, you should check before signing up to any breakdown/recovery scheme that they operate a system of this type and make sure that you're registered for priority response.

For people with illness-related disabilities, it's also worth finding out if the breakdown/recovery scheme will recover your vehicle in the event that you become too ill to continue your journey. Some schemes won't recover a driveable vehicle irrespective of the health or condition of the rider/driver.

Emergency telephones

These telephones are connected to control centres and are on most stretches of motorway at one-mile intervals. Look for a telephone symbol and arrow on marker posts 100 metres (328 feet) apart along the hard shoulder.

The arrow directs you to the nearest phone on your side of the carriageway. Walk to the telephone, keeping on the inside of the hard shoulder.

REMEMBER, never cross the carriageway or an exit or entry slip road to reach a phone or for any other purpose.

Using the emergency telephone

The telephone connects you to a control centre, which will put you through to a breakdown service. In the case of criminal matters, the control centre will reroute the call to the police.

In the interests of safety, always face the traffic when you speak on the telephone.

You'll be asked for

- the number on the telephone, which gives your precise location
- details of your vehicle and your membership details, if you belong to one of the motoring organisations
- details of the fault.

If you're a vulnerable motorcyclist, such as a woman travelling alone, make this clear to the operator. You'll be told approximately how long you'll have to wait.

Face the traffic when using an emergency telephone.

263

Mobile phones

If you're unable to use an emergency telephone, use a mobile phone if you have one. However, before you call, make sure that you can give precise details of your location. Marker posts on the side of the hard shoulder identify your location and you should provide these details when you call.

Waiting for the emergency services

Wait on the bank near your vehicle, so you can see the emergency services arriving. Motorway deaths have been caused by vehicles being driven into people on the hard shoulder.

If you're approached by anyone you don't recognise as a member of the emergency services, think carefully before you speak to them. If they try to speak to you, ask for some identification and tell them that the police or control centre have been told and the emergency services are coming.

A traffic officer or a person claiming to be from the emergency services should have

- an identity card

- your details: your name and information about the breakdown.

Find out what to do if you break down on a motorway at this link.

surviVegroup.org/pages/safety-information/stopping-on-the-hard-shoulder

Rejoining the motorway

Use the hard shoulder to build up speed before joining the other traffic when it's safe to do so. Don't try to move out from behind another vehicle or force your way into the stream of traffic.

Remember to switch off your hazard warning lights before moving off.

Motorways at night

> If you've just left a well-lit service area, give your eyes time to adjust to the darkness.

Use your headlights

Always use your headlights, even on motorways that are lit. Use dipped beam if you're likely to dazzle drivers ahead or oncoming drivers, particularly on a left-hand curve.

If you're dazzled
You may have to slow down, but don't brake too hard; there might be a vehicle behind you.

Judging speed

It's harder to judge speed and distance both on a motorway and at night.

If you change lanes to overtake, or to leave the motorway, use your indicators earlier and give yourself more time.

Reflective road studs

These can help you determine the road layout. Their positions are as follows.

- Red – between the hard shoulder and the carriageway.
- White – between lanes.
- Amber – between the edge of the carriageway and the central reservation.
- Green – between the carriageway and slip-road exits and entrances.
- Fluorescent green/yellow – at contraflow systems and roadworks.

 Roadworks

Incidents can happen at roadworks. Obey all signs, including speed-limit signs.

Approaching roadworks

- Reduce speed in good time when warned by advance warning signs, gantry signs or flashing signals – don't leave everything to the last minute, as this can greatly increase the chance of mistakes and incidents.
- Get into the lane indicated for use by your vehicle in good time.
- Where lanes are restricted, merge in turn.

- When you drop your speed, it may seem as if you're travelling more slowly than you really are. It's important to observe the speed limit and not just slow down to the speed that feels safe to you.

- Look out for road workers who are placing or removing signs. They might need to cross the carriageway, especially when temporary barriers and cones are being set up or taken down.

Travelling through roadworks

- Obey all speed limits – they're there for a reason. Roadworks are complicated areas and you'll need more time to spot hazards, for your own safety and the safety of road workers.

- If all road users observe the speed limits, it helps to keep traffic moving and prevent 'bunching up'. This is good for journey times and the environment.

- Keep the correct separation distance from the vehicle ahead; you'll need time to brake if the vehicle in front stops suddenly.

- Avoid sharp braking and sudden changes of direction.

- Don't change lanes when signs tell you to stay in your lane.

- Don't let your attention wander; there may be road workers in unexpected places, and they can be difficult to spot in cluttered areas.

> **REMEMBER**, people may be working at roadworks sites and their safety is at risk if you don't follow the advice above.

Exiting roadworks

Stay within the speed limit even when you're leaving the coned area. There may be road workers' vehicles leaving the roadworks at this point. Even if you see the road worker, remember that they may not have seen you. Don't speed up until you're clear of the roadworks.

Mobile roadworks

Minor maintenance work may sometimes be carried out without the need for major lane closures. Slow-moving or stationary works vehicles, with a large arrow on the back of the vehicle, are used to divert traffic to the right or left as appropriate.

There are no cones when these vehicles are being used.

Contraflow systems

These are temporary systems where traffic travelling in opposite directions shares the same carriageway. They allow traffic to keep moving during repairs or alterations on the other carriageway.

The lanes are often narrower than normal lanes. Red-and-white marker posts separate traffic travelling in opposite directions, and fluorescent or reflective bright green/yellow road studs often replace normal ones.

Contraflow systems may also be found on other roads carrying fast-moving traffic.

Watch out for

- lane-change signs
- vehicles broken down ahead – there's often no hard shoulder
- vehicles braking ahead – keep your distance.

(→) Traffic officers

Working in partnership with the police, traffic officers are extra eyes and ears on most motorways and some 'A' class roads in England only. They're a highly trained and highly visible service patrolling the motorway to help keep traffic moving and to make your journey as safe and reliable as possible.

Traffic officers wear a full uniform, including a high-visibility orange-and-yellow jacket, and drive a high-visibility vehicle with yellow-and-black chequered markings.

Every traffic officer has a unique identification number and photographic identity card. They normally patrol in pairs. The vehicles contain a variety of equipment for use on the motorway, including temporary road signs, lights, cones, debris removal tools and a first-aid kit.

Role of traffic officers

They

- help broken-down motorists to arrange recovery
- offer safety advice to motorists
- clear debris from the carriageway
- undertake high-visibility patrols
- support the police and emergency services during incidents
- provide mobile or temporary road closures
- manage diversion routes caused by an incident.

If you have an emergency or break down on the motorway, the best action to take is to use an emergency roadside telephone.

Emergency roadside telephones are answered by operators located in a regional control centre. Control-centre operators are able to monitor any stranded motorists on closed-circuit television (CCTV) screens and despatch the nearest available traffic-officer patrol to assist.

Powers of traffic officers

Unlike the police, traffic officers don't have any enforcement powers. However, they're able to stop and direct anyone travelling on the motorway. It's an offence not to comply with the directions given by a traffic officer (refer to The Highway Code, rules 107 and 108).

Extent of scheme

Seven regional control centres, managed by Highways England, are able to despatch traffic officers to any motorway in England.

Section twelve

⊕ All-weather riding

This section covers

- Your motorcycle
- Weather and vision
- Riding on wet roads
- Riding in fog
- Riding in cold weather
- Riding in windy weather
- Riding in sunshine and hot weather

⊕ Your motorcycle

Whatever the weather, make sure your motorcycle is in good condition. It should be checked and serviced regularly. Contending with the elements can be difficult, but having to contend with a poorly performing motorcycle at the same time is an extra difficulty you can do without.

Tyres

Tyres are an important safety item; they should be checked regularly.

Check for

- tread depth
- pressure
- objects stuck in the tyre
- cuts or damage.

Your safety could depend on the condition of your tyres. Always make sure that they have sufficient tread and are correctly inflated. Incorrect tyre pressures can cause loss of stability, reduced grip and increased wear.

Brakes

Check that your brakes are in good condition. Wet weather will increase your stopping distance, even with perfect brakes.

Electrics

Motorcycle electrical systems are exposed to the elements. Damp or wet weather may affect your ignition system and may cause

- starting problems
- the engine to misfire.

A misfiring engine will cause loss of power and may stop running altogether.

Keep your battery in good condition. In cold weather, an electric starter places big demands on the battery, so it's important to check your battery regularly.

Lights

Always keep your lights, indicators and reflectors clean. Dirty lights can seriously reduce how far you can see, as well as affecting how clearly other people can see you and your signals. Check your lights and bulbs regularly.

⊙ Weather and vision

The single biggest danger to any rider is being unable to see properly. You won't be able to make the right decisions if you can't see the road clearly. Remember also that, at night, the reflection from wet roads will make it difficult to see unlit objects.

Rain

In heavy rain, your visor or goggles can easily mist up, and this can affect your view of the road. If you can't see clearly, stop and demist your visor or goggles. It's a good idea to carry a cloth with you especially for this purpose.

If you wear glasses, it may be that they too have misted over. Don't be tempted to ride without your glasses if you need them to bring your eyesight up to the legal requirement.

Some modern helmets have air vents to help prevent fogging up, and anti-fog products are also available.

Keeping dry

If you allow yourself to get wet, you'll also get cold. Being cold and wet can seriously reduce your ability to concentrate.

Proper motorcycle clothing is available that will keep you dry in the heaviest downpour. This is a must if you intend to ride in bad weather.

Fog

When riding in fog, you may have the combined problems of

- fogging up on the inside of your visor or goggles, and
- misting over on the outside of your visor or goggles.

Water droplets can form evenly across the outside of your visor or goggles. This can be difficult to detect, because it appears that the loss of vision is being caused by the density of the fog, rather than this mist of water droplets. Wipe your visor or goggles frequently to prevent this mist from obscuring your view of the road.

In freezing fog, the mist build-up can quickly freeze over. Once it's frozen, you'll have to stop and de-ice your visor or goggles to restore a clear view.

Being seen

Making yourself visible to other road users is important at all times. In the rain and fog it's especially so, because of the reduction in visibility.

Wear bright, high-visibility clothing and keep your headlights on dipped beam.

⊛ Riding on wet roads

Wet roads reduce tyre grip. Give yourself plenty of time and room to slow down and stop. Keep well back from other vehicles.

On a wet road, you should allow at least double the braking distance that you'd allow on a dry road.

After a spell of dry weather, rain on the road can make the surface even more slippery. Take extra care, especially when cornering.

Be aware that different road surfaces might affect the grip of your tyres. Surfaces to be wary of include

- metal drain covers
- painted road markings

- tar banding
- patched areas
- where mud or muck has been dropped. You should also look out for the cause of this, such as slow agricultural machines, dairy cattle, lorries, or heavy plant where civil engineering projects are under way
- where diesel fuel has been spilt. This is commonly found outside filling stations, on roundabouts and at bus stops. It may be visible as a rainbow-coloured film on the road surface
- where leaves have fallen in autumn.

These surfaces need extra care when cornering or braking.

Surface water

When the rain is very heavy, or if the road has poor drainage, you'll have to deal with surface water.

If you ride through surface water too fast, your tyres might not be able to displace the water quickly enough. A thin film of water can then build up between the tyre and the road, so that the tyre loses contact with the road and all grip is lost. This effect is called 'aquaplaning'. High speed and worn tyres increase the risk of aquaplaning.

To avoid aquaplaning

- Keep your speed down.
- Avoid riding through water pooling on the road surface, if you can do so safely.

If you feel your motorcycle start to aquaplane, ease off the throttle. Don't brake or turn the steering until grip is restored.

Try not to splash pedestrians by riding through pools of water close to the kerb.

Heavy rain and surface water make it easier to skid and make aquaplaning a possibility.

Brakes

As well as reducing tyre grip, water can reduce the effectiveness of your brakes, meaning that it will take longer to stop. You should allow for this and keep your speed down.

If the surface is good but wet, you should

- aim to brake when the machine is in its most stable position; that is, upright and moving straight ahead
- apply the front brake slightly before the rear brake. Spread the braking effort evenly between the front and rear brakes.

Floods

Before you ride through flood water, stop and assess how deep the water is. Roads that flood regularly may have depth gauges. You can check the depth of the water on these.

If the water seems too deep, turn back and go around the flood by another route. It may take a little longer but it's better than becoming stranded in the flood.

If the water isn't too deep, ride through slowly and

- keep in a low gear
- keep your engine running fast enough to prevent water from entering the exhaust
- try to ride where the water is shallowest. Because of the camber on roads, this is most likely to be in the centre (or 'crown') of the road. Watch for oncoming vehicles that may be doing the same thing
- test your brakes when you're out of the water.

Crossing fords

A ford is a place where a stream crosses a road, and so the road surface is also a stream bed. It may

- be very uneven, with loose stones
- have a slippery coating on many of its surfaces
- have a strong current.

All of these can make riding through a ford a very hazardous activity.

The depth of water at fords varies with the weather but is usually greater in winter. There may be a depth gauge that tells you how deep the water is.

If the water isn't too deep for your motorcycle, cross using the same technique you would use for a flood. Remember to test your brakes after you cross. There might be a notice reminding you to do so.

Don't try to displace the water by charging at it. This may mean that

- your motorcycle stalls
- you lose control, resulting in you falling off, injury to yourself, your passenger or another road user, and maybe even damage to property
- you end up blocking the road.

Test your brakes

Water can reduce the effectiveness of your brakes, so test your brakes when you've passed through water on the road. When you've ridden through safely, first check your mirrors to make sure it's clear behind and then try your brakes.

If they don't work properly, it will help to dry them out if you apply light pressure to the brake lever/pedal while riding along slowly. Don't ride at speed until you're sure that the brakes are working normally.

Riding in fog

Fog is one of the most dangerous weather conditions. An incident involving one vehicle can quickly involve many others, especially if they're travelling too close to one another.

Motorway pile-ups in fog have sometimes involved dozens of vehicles. All too often there's a loss of life or serious injury that could easily have been prevented.

REMEMBER, if the fog is thick and you can see the rear lights of the vehicle ahead, then you may be too close to stop in an emergency.

Observe the obvious

If it's foggy and you can only see a short distance ahead, you should start thinking about how the conditions will affect your riding.

Do you need to ride?

Take alternative transport or postpone your journey, if at all possible. If you must ride, give yourself time to prepare.

Check all the lights on your motorcycle, clean your visor or goggles, and make sure you've made every effort to be as visible to other road users as you possibly can. This should include wiping your number plates. Remember that foggy conditions mean that your journey will take longer, so try to allow yourself more time and plan rest stops where appropriate.

Use of lights

When riding in fog in daylight, you **MUST** use dipped headlights if visibility is seriously reduced, because they'll be seen from a much greater distance than sidelights.

Don't use main beam when you're in fog, because

- the fog reflects the light and can dazzle you, reducing your view even further
- you may dazzle other drivers.

High-intensity rear fog light

If your motorcycle has a high-intensity rear fog light, use it only in fog, when visibility is less than 100 metres (328 feet).

You **MUST** switch it off when visibility improves – it's the law. Using it at other times, such as in the rain, can dazzle drivers behind you.

Adjust your lights

Change your lighting with the conditions. For example, when you're queuing in traffic and the driver behind has already seen you, it can be helpful to switch off your rear fog light temporarily to avoid dazzling them.

Visibility

Poor visibility is frustrating and a strain on the eyes. Your ability to anticipate is dangerously restricted.

It's also much more difficult to judge distances and speed in fog when outlines become confusing. You can easily become disoriented – especially on an unfamiliar road.

If you find yourself in fog

- Slow down so that you can stop within the distance you can see to be clear.
- Use your dipped headlights.
- Keep your visor or goggles clear.
- Keep a safe distance from the vehicle in front.
- Use your rear fog light (if fitted) when visibility falls below 100 metres (328 feet).

Fog patches

The density of fog varies. Sometimes the fog is patchy. One moment it can be fairly clear, the next extremely dense. Avoid the temptation to speed up between the patches.

Positioning

Try to keep a central position between lane lines or road studs. Don't mix up lane lines and centre lines.

Riding too close to the centre of the road could mean you're dangerously near someone coming the other way, who might be doing the same thing. Riding on the centre line as a means of finding your way is extremely dangerous.

Road markings

Dipped headlights will pick out reflective road studs, but it isn't as easy to recognise other road markings when riding in fog. Explanations of the different colours of road studs are given in section 11.

Following another vehicle

Slow down and leave plenty of room to stop. There may be something ahead that you can't possibly see until you're too close to it.

You must leave enough space to react and brake in case the vehicle in front has to stop suddenly. You may not see or recognise that the vehicle ahead is braking, or has stopped, as soon as you would in clear weather.

Remember, the road surface is often wet and slippery in fog; you need to be able to brake safely.

Overtaking

Overtaking in fog can be particularly dangerous. You could well find that visibility ahead is much worse than you thought, and you won't be able to see oncoming traffic soon enough.

Never begin to overtake unless you can clearly see that it's safe to do so. There won't be many such opportunities when riding in mist or fog.

Junctions

Dealing with junctions in fog needs particular care, especially when turning right.

You should

- listen for approaching traffic
- start indicating as early as you can
- be aware that other road users may not be using their lights
- use the horn if you feel it will help.

Don't turn or emerge until you're absolutely sure it's safe.

Parking

Never park on a road in the fog if you can avoid it. Find an off-street parking place.

However, if it's unavoidable, always leave your parking lights on.

Breakdowns

If you break down, get your motorcycle off the road if you possibly can. Inform the police and make arrangements to remove it as soon as possible if it creates an obstruction.

Never leave your motorcycle without warning lights of some kind, or on the wrong side of the road.

⊕ Riding in cold weather

If you get cold when riding

- your concentration will suffer
- your ability to control your machine will be affected
- your enjoyment of motorcycling will be reduced.

Keeping warm can be a problem. However, motorcycle clothing is available that will keep you warm in very low temperatures. This clothing isn't cheap, but it's essential if you want to ride in cold weather.

The cold will probably affect your hands and feet first. Don't continue if you lose feeling in your fingers or toes. Stop from time to time to warm up.

Stop to warm up before you lose feeling in your fingers. You won't be able to operate the controls properly if your fingers become numb.

Snow and ice

It's better not to ride at all in conditions of snow and ice. If you must travel in these conditions, keep to the main roads. These are more likely to be clear and treated with salt or other de-icer.

When you're riding on snow or ice, your motorcycle's tyres have reduced grip on the road. Keep your speed down and take great care when

- accolerating
- braking
- cornering.

> **REMEMBER**, using the controls gently and carefully will help you maintain control.

Snow
In falling snow, use your dipped headlights and keep your visor or goggles clear. Snow will quickly cover road signs and markings. Be aware of the danger this creates.

Snow can also build up over your headlights and indicators as you ride. This will quickly reduce their effectiveness. If this happens, stop frequently to clear the snow away.

Ice

Overnight freezing can result in an icy surface, especially on less frequently used roads. Look for signs of frost on verges, etc.

It's even more dangerous when the roads are just beginning to freeze or thaw. The combination of water and ice adds up to an extremely slippery surface.

You should watch for areas where ice may linger after it has cleared elsewhere. These places may include

- areas of shade caused by features such as trees, hedges and buildings
- exposed roads where wind chill keeps the ground temperature low
- low-lying areas where cold air gathers
- shaded hills and slopes.

Other road users may not appreciate how severely the conditions are affecting you. If someone is following too closely, pull over and let them go past.

Black ice

Black ice is very dangerous. It forms when droplets of water freeze on a normally good, skid-resistant surface. Black ice is so dangerous because it's almost invisible.

In wintry conditions, if the road looks wet but you can't hear tyre noise as you would on a wet road, suspect black ice.

If your machine is left out overnight and it's covered in frost or ice in the morning, this is an obvious clue that the roads may also be affected.

⊕ Riding in windy weather

A strong gust of wind from one side can suddenly blow you off course. You're likely to be affected by these side winds

- as you pass gateways or gaps in hedges
- as you pass gaps in buildings
- as you pass high-sided vehicles
- on exposed roads.

When it's windy, keep your speed down so that you remain in control. Look ahead and anticipate places where side winds may affect you.

Side winds can affect other road users too. The most vulnerable include

- cyclists
- drivers of high-sided vehicles
- other motorcyclists
- drivers of vehicles towing trailers or caravans.

Take care and allow extra room.

A strong gust of wind from your left could blow you towards oncoming traffic.

⊙ Riding in sunshine and hot weather

Motorcycling is probably at its best during warm, dry weather. However, even this type of weather brings challenges for the rider.

Visors and goggles

There are generally more flies and insects about in hot weather, and they can soon cause a dirty and smeary visor or goggles. This can reduce your view of the road, especially at night, and it worsens the effects of glare.

Always keep your visor or goggles clean and free from smears (see section 4).

Dust and dirt can cause tiny scratches on visors and goggles. These scratches build up over time. Replace your visor or goggles if they become heavily scratched.

Clothing

Never be tempted to ride without protective clothing, even on the hottest days. You could be horribly injured by even the most minor incident.

Some riders have lightweight protective summer clothing. This will help to keep you both cooler and protected.

It's important that you keep hydrated in hot weather – especially when travelling abroad, in hot countries. Make sure you've had something to drink before you start out, and carry water with you. It's essential to schedule proper breaks to eat, drink and rest if you're driving long distances.

Glare

Constant sun in your eyes can be exhausting on a long journey and may well affect your concentration. Even if you don't feel the need, wearing sunglasses can help to reduce glare and ease the strain on your eyes. This is especially important if you're riding abroad, where conditions are hotter and the sunlight brighter than you may be used to.

If the roads are wet, reflected glare seriously reduces your ability to see. Reduce speed and take extra care.

Low sun both dazzles and casts long shadows, which can conceal hazards.

Low-angle sun

Glare can be worse in the winter, when the sun is low in the sky. Wearing sunglasses or using an approved tinted visor can help to reduce the glare. If you're affected, slow down so that you can stop within the distance you can see. Avoid looking directly into the sun.

You **MUST NOT** wear tinted glasses, visors or goggles in the dark or in conditions of poor visibility.

Road surface

During a long spell of hot, dry weather, the road surface will become coated with rubber, particularly at

- junctions
- bends
- roundabouts.

When it rains after such a dry spell, the road will be unusually slippery. Look out for shiny surfaces.

Loose chippings

Many highway authorities replace the granite-chipping road surfaces during the summer. While this work is being carried out, you may have to ride on temporary road surfaces. These can be very rough. You also need to watch for humps at the beginning and end of the temporary surface.

You should

- take extra care
- observe the special warning speed limits
- keep well back from the vehicle in front.

When a road has been resurfaced with chippings, it has a very loose surface for several days. Loose chippings will reduce your tyres' grip on the road. When riding on loose chippings, take care when

- accelerating
- braking
- cornering.

Watch for the warning signs and keep your speed down. Flying stone chips can cause

- expensive damage to your vehicle
- eye injury if you ride without goggles or with your visor raised
- serious injury to pedestrians and other road users.

If you park on soft tarmac, the stand can sink into the road surface.

Soft tarmac

During long periods of hot weather, many tarmac road surfaces become extremely soft. Take care when braking and cornering.

Melted tar can reduce tyre grip and can lead to skidding.

→ Riding at night

This section covers

- Seeing at night
- Lights
- Being seen
- Built-up areas
- Overtaking or following at night
- Parking at night
- Meeting other vehicles

⊕ Seeing at night

Riding at night is another aspect of motorcycling that demands special techniques and precautions.

If you find that you can't see so well in the dark, it might be that you need to book an appointment with an optician for an eye test.

How far can you see?

Test yourself in a suitable place.

Pick an object within the range of your lights and see if you can stop by the time you reach it. You'll be surprised how difficult this is with dipped lights on an unlit road. It shows that you should take a good look before you dip your lights.

Lighter-coloured objects are easier to see at night.

Adjusting to darkness

Give your eyes a minute or two to adjust to the darkness, particularly when you're coming out of a brightly lit area or building.

To help you see at night, you should keep your goggles or visor clean. Scratches on either can cause dazzle from approaching traffic. If your goggles or visor become scratched, you should replace them.

If you're riding in the dark, don't wear

- sunglasses
- tinted goggles
- a tinted visor.

 REMEMBER, when you leave a brightly lit service area, your eyes will need time to adjust to the darkness.

 Lights

To help other road users to see you, ride with your headlights on dipped beam at all times – even in good daylight.

In the dark, your vehicle lights are the most important source of information both for you and for other road users.

- Keep your lights clean.
- Check all your lights before any journey.
- Fix any lighting fault immediately, for your own safety and the safety of others. Carry spare bulbs if applicable.
- Practise operating the light switches, so that you can find them easily in the dark.
- Remember that the extra weight of a pillion passenger or a load could cause your headlights to aim higher than normal. This could dazzle other road users and reduce the effectiveness of your lights. Adjust your headlights to address this.

Using dipped beam

You must use dipped headlights

- at night when the street lighting is poor; for example, if the street lights are more than 185 metres (600 feet) apart
- in poor visibility
- at night on all other roads, including motorways.

Using main beam

Use your headlights on main beam in any conditions where the main beam will help you to see without dazzling other road users.

When your headlights are on main beam, the blue main-beam warning light will glow.

Dipping your headlights

Dip your main beam

- in the face of oncoming traffic
- when approaching traffic from behind.

Don't dazzle other road users – you could cause an incident.

When you dip your headlights

- you'll see less of the road ahead
- you should slow down, so that you can stop within the distance you can see.

⊕ Being seen

At night, it's more difficult for other road users to see you in good time. In congested urban areas, a single motorcycle headlight can get lost in the background of distracting lights.

Although bright fluorescent clothing is highly effective at increasing your visibility in daylight, it's less effective in the dark, when reflective material should be used. Reflective material works by reflecting the light shone onto it (such as headlights). This makes it easier for others to see you at night.

Reflective material can be worn in various ways, such as

- reflective strips or panels integrated into motorcycle clothing
- high-visibility overjackets or tabards
- a 'Sam Browne' belt.

Reflectors are fitted to all motorcycles by the manufacturers. You should make sure they're clean. You may also fit additional reflective panels or tape to further increase your visibility.

Be aware of the difficulty other road users might have in seeing you, and

- ride with dipped headlights on (unless you need to use main beam)
- keep your lights clean and working correctly
- keep your reflective number plate clean.

Wearing bright clothing with reflective panels makes it easier for others to see you, especially from the side, such as here at a road junction.

⊕ Built-up areas

Always use dipped headlights in built-up areas at night. It helps others to see you.

In areas where street lights cause patches of shadow, or where street lights are dimmed or turned off, watch out for pedestrians (especially those in dark clothes), who can be difficult to see.

Remember to

- be on the alert for pedestrians
- approach pedestrian crossings at a speed at which you can stop safely if necessary
- watch for cyclists and joggers.

> **REMEMBER**, after it has rained, the reflections from wet surfaces will make it difficult to see unlit objects.

The bright lights in a busy street can be distracting and make it difficult to see hazards that are poorly lit.

Noise at night

Keep all noise to a minimum and try not to disturb residents, who may be asleep.

- Don't rev your engine unnecessarily.
- Take extra care when setting or disarming any anti-theft alarm on your motorcycle.

Using the horn at night

You **MUST NOT** use your horn between 11.30 pm and 7.00 am in a built-up area (except to avoid danger from a moving vehicle).

If you need to warn other road users of your presence at night, flash your headlights.

⊕ Overtaking or following at night

You'll need to take extra care before attempting to overtake at night. It's more difficult because you can see less. Only overtake if you can see that the road ahead will remain clear until after you've finished the manoeuvre. Don't overtake if there's a chance you're approaching

- a road junction or bend
- a dip in the road
- the brow of a bridge or hill, except on a dual carriageway
- a pedestrian crossing
- double white lines

or if there's likely to be

- a vehicle overtaking or turning right
- any other potential hazard.

Stay clear and dip

Make sure you don't get too close to the vehicle ahead, and always dip your headlights so that you don't cause dazzle.

Your light beam should fall short of the rear of the vehicle in front. Remember your separation distance.

On a dual carriageway or motorway where it's possible to overtake, don't use main beam in the face of oncoming drivers.

If you're being overtaken

Dip your headlights as soon as the vehicle starts to pass you, to avoid causing glare in the mirrors of the overtaking vehicle.

Don't dazzle the driver in front. Hold back so that the beam of your headlights falls short of their vehicle.

⊕ Parking at night

>
>
> **FACTS** Cars, light goods vehicles (2500 kg or less laden weight), invalid carriages and motorcycles can park without lights on roads with a speed limit of 30 mph (48 km/h) or less. They must comply with any parking restrictions, and not park within 10 metres (32 feet) of a junction.
>
> They must also be parked parallel to, and close to, the side of the road or in a designated parking place and facing in the direction of the traffic flow.

If you have to park on any other road, you should never

- leave your motorcycle without parking lights unless a sign indicates that lights aren't required. It would be better to get it off the road altogether
- leave your vehicle standing on the right-hand side of the road, except in a one-way street.

Always switch your headlights off when you stop, even for a short while. It's an offence to leave them on when parked. The fixed glare can be very dazzling – especially if, for any reason, you've parked on the offside of the road, facing oncoming traffic.

⊕ Meeting other vehicles

Another vehicle's lights can tell you in which direction they're heading and can give you an idea of their speed. Oncoming lights should raise a number of questions in your mind, such as

- How far away is the vehicle and how fast is it moving?
- Should I slow down while we pass each other?
- How soon should I dip my headlights?
- How far ahead can I see before I dip?
- Before I dip, is there anything on my side of the road
  - that I might endanger?
  - that might endanger me?

  Examples include a stationary vehicle, a cyclist, a pedestrian, or an unlit skip.

Headlights on main beam

When your headlights are on main beam

- dip early enough to avoid dazzling oncoming drivers, but not too early
- check the left-hand verge before you dip.

If you're dazzled

If the headlights of oncoming vehicles dazzle you, slow down and, if necessary, stop. Don't look directly at oncoming headlights.

Don't retaliate by leaving your headlights on main beam and dazzling the oncoming driver.

On a left-hand bend
Dip earlier. Your headlights will point directly towards the eyes of anyone coming towards you as you ride around the bend.

On a right-hand bend
Your headlights will point at the left-hand edge of the road but the lights of approaching traffic will be more likely to dazzle you.

You're more likely to be dazzled by the lights of an oncoming vehicle on a right-hand bend or on the crest of a hill.

Section fourteen

⊙ Passengers and loads

This section covers

- Carrying a passenger
- Carrying a load
- Sidecar outfits
- Towing a trailer

⊙ Carrying a passenger

Riding with a passenger or a load can call for adjustments to your machine, as well as to your riding. You should check your vehicle handbook for information about the maximum weight your machine is rated to carry. This will include figures for the rider, carrying a pillion passenger and even towing a trailer.

Riders with disabilities should be aware that, when carrying a pillion passenger and/or heavy luggage on a two-wheeled vehicle, they'll be required to stabilise the vehicle with considerable extra weight whenever it comes to a stop. This isn't only a potential problem for people with disabilities affecting the weight-bearing strength of a leg; it can also be hazardous for people who have disabilities affecting the strength or mobility of an arm, or the mobility of the hips. Riders must be certain that they're able to cope easily with the extra load of a pillion passenger and/or luggage, rather than putting themselves, the passenger and other road users at unnecessary risk.

Legal requirements

You **MUST NOT** carry a pillion passenger unless

- you've passed your practical motorcycle test
- you hold a full licence for the category of motorcycle you're riding.

To carry a passenger, your motorcycle should have

- rear footrests
- a proper passenger seat.

Motorcycle adjustments

To cope with the extra load of a pillion passenger, you should

- inflate the tyres according to the manufacturer's instructions
- adjust the preload on the rear shock absorbers to allow for the extra weight (see your vehicle handbook for details)
- adjust the headlight aim, if necessary.

Checking motorcycle tyre pressure.

Adjusting the rear shock-absorber preload setting.

Passengers

If your passenger has never ridden pillion before, or you doubt their experience, instruct them to

- sit astride the machine, facing forwards
- wear an approved motorcycle helmet, properly fastened
- keep both feet on the passenger footrests until they dismount
- keep a light but firm hold on your waist or the passenger grab handle (if fitted)
- lean with you while going around bends or corners.

Instruct your passenger not to

- look behind or signal for you
- lean to the side to see ahead. This might affect your balance and stability.

Passenger's clothing

Your passenger's clothing should be

- weatherproof and protective
- bright and, if riding at night, reflective.

Don't allow your passenger to wear a scarf or belt loosely fastened. These can get tangled in the wheel or drive chain and cause serious injury.

Riding techniques

Until you get used to carrying a passenger, ride with extra care. The presence of the passenger will affect

- your balance, especially at low speeds
- your ability to stop. The extra weight may increase your stopping distance. Allow a bigger gap when following another vehicle
- your acceleration. You'll be slower to get moving, so allow more room when emerging at junctions.

Don't

- carry a child on a motorcycle unless they can safely use the footrests and handholds, and they're wearing a properly fitting helmet
- ask your passenger to look behind or signal for you
- accept any road or traffic information from your passenger without verifying it.

⊙ Carrying a load

All riders are allowed to carry loads but it's the rider's responsibility to ensure that the

- load is secure
- motorcycle isn't overloaded.

There are various ways to carry loads, including panniers, top boxes, tank bags and luggage racks.

Panniers

Two types of pannier are available: rigidly fixed and throw-over saddlebag.

Whichever type you use, always make sure that you load the panniers evenly. Uneven loading can lead to loss of stability.

Top box

A top box is fastened onto a rack behind the seat. It's easy and quick to use, but it has its limitations. The weight is carried high up and at the very back of the machine. Don't carry heavy loads in a top box, because this can

- reduce stability
- cause low-speed wobble
- cause high-speed weave.

Tank bag

A tank bag is fastened on top of the fuel tank (or dummy tank) and can carry large loads. Take care that the tank bag doesn't interfere with your ability to steer.

Luggage rack

Make sure that any items strapped to a luggage rack are securely fastened. A loose load could become tangled in the rear wheel and cause an incident.

Adjusting your motorcycle

Make any necessary adjustments to the suspension, tyres and lights.

When riding with a load, give yourself the chance to get used to the extra weight. If the load is unevenly distributed and your machine is unbalanced, stop and rearrange the load.

⊙ Sidecar outfits

If you want to fit a sidecar, you should

- ask your dealer whether your machine is suitable
- make sure that, after fitting, the sidecar is fixed correctly to the mounting points
- fit it on the left-hand side of the machine if the machine was registered on or after 1 August 1981.

Motorcycles and sidecar outfits need a very different technique from solo motorcycles.

Aligning the sidecar

Make sure that the motorcycle and sidecar are correctly aligned. If they aren't, the outfit will be difficult to control and probably dangerous.

Riding techniques

You must adopt a different technique when riding a motorcycle with a sidecar. Keep your speed down until you've become used to the outfit.

On bends and when turning, the sidecar outfit must be steered, because you can't lean the machine over. This requires a deliberate push or pull on the handlebars.

On left-hand bends, the sidecar wheel will tend to lift as the weight is thrown outwards. This calls for special care and control.

Braking

Unless a brake is fitted to the sidecar wheel, the outfit will tend to pull to the right under heavy braking.

The extra weight of the sidecar may increase the overall stopping distance.

⊕ Towing a trailer

You may only tow a trailer behind your motorcycle if

- you have a full motorcycle licence
- your machine has an engine capacity exceeding 125 cc
- the trailer doesn't exceed 1 metre (3 feet 3 inches) in width
- the distance between the rear axle of the motorcycle and the rear of the trailer is less than 2.5 metres (about 8 feet)
- the motorcycle is clearly marked with its kerbside weight
- the trailer is clearly marked with its unladen weight
- the laden weight of the trailer doesn't exceed 150 kg or two-thirds of the kerbside weight of the motorcycle, whichever is less.

You can't tow

- more than one trailer
- a trailer with a passenger in it.

When you tow a trailer, remember that

- your stopping distance may be increased
- any load in the trailer must be secure
- the trailer must be fitted to the machine correctly
- you must obey the following speed limits, which apply to all vehicles towing trailers
    - 30 mph (48 km/h) in built-up areas
    - 50 mph (80 km/h) on single carriageways
    - 60 mph (96 km/h) on dual carriageways or motorways.

Section fifteen

→ Basic maintenance

This section covers

- Regular checks
- Engine
- Suspension, steering and wheels
- Controls
- Electrical systems

⊕ Regular checks

A motorcycle needs routine maintenance to keep it in a roadworthy condition. Learning how to carry out routine maintenance yourself will save you time and money.

Many routine maintenance jobs are straightforward and are explained in the vehicle handbook. More difficult tasks may need to be referred to your dealer. Rider training courses may include some mechanical instruction and advice on maintenance.

You **MUST** make sure your lights and number plates are kept clean at all times. Also, you should check the following items on a regular basis.

Engine

- fuel
- oil (engine, gearbox and final drive)
- coolant (liquid-cooled engines)
- air filter.

Suspension and steering

- suspension
- steering-head bearings
- wheels
- tyres.

Controls

- brakes
- clutch
- throttle.

Electrical systems

- battery
- lights
- horn
- indicators.

Disabled riders

Some disabled riders may find it difficult to kneel, squat or bend down to carry out basic maintenance tasks. There are a number of motorcycle lifting devices that can be used to raise the motorcycle to a height where it can be worked on comfortably and safely. You should check that the maximum safe lifting capacity is suitable for your machine before buying or using this type of equipment.

People with disabilities involving paralysis or affecting the mobility and/or dexterity of hands or fingers may find that a good-quality pressure washer with a range of attachments is helpful in cleaning some of the less accessible parts of motorcycles and trikes.

 # Engine

A properly maintained engine will

- start more easily
- use less fuel
- be more reliable
- give optimum performance
- have lower exhaust emissions.

Items that will affect the engine performance include

- spark plugs
- ignition settings
- air filter
- carburettor settings
- valve clearances.

If you aren't confident in your ability to maintain the engine, entrust the work to your dealer.

Fuel

Many modern motorcycles are fitted
with a fuel gauge and a warning light
that flashes when the petrol level is
low. If your motorcycle doesn't have a
fuel gauge, you'll have to remove the
filler cap to check how much fuel
you have.

Some motorcycles have a reserve
supply of petrol, which is accessed
by setting the fuel tap to a 'reserve' position. The amount of petrol held in this
reserve varies by make and model, but it's typically enough to ride 20–30 miles.

When the main tank becomes empty, the engine will lose power and may
'cough' or even cut out altogether. The fuel tap needs to be moved to the
'reserve' position and there may be a slight delay before the fuel reaches the
engine. This could be hazardous in certain circumstances, so it's advisable to
refuel before the reserve level is reached.

If you do use the reserve, remember to turn the fuel tap back to the normal
'on' position when you refuel.

For motorcycles that don't have a fuel gauge, it's a good idea to reset the trip
meter when you refuel. You can use the mileage to work out when you need
to refuel again.

Types of engine

Two types of petrol engine are fitted to motorcycles

* two-stroke

* four-stroke.

If you don't know which type of engine is fitted to your motorcycle, check the
vehicle handbook or ask your dealer.

Two-stroke engines

A two-stroke engine runs on a combined petrol/oil mixture. A special two-
stroke oil needs to be combined with the petrol in a ratio determined by the
manufacturer. This ratio may be 20:1, for example.

Two-stroke oil is combined with the petrol by either

- directly adding the oil to the petrol when refuelling

- adding two-stroke oil to a special oil tank. This oil is then automatically mixed with the petrol as it's fed to the engine.

When refuelling a motorcycle with a two-stroke engine, you must remember to add/check the two-stroke oil.

Four-stroke engines

It's important that you use the correct grade of petrol for your engine. Most modern four-stroke motorcycle engines run on unleaded fuel, but older models may require lead-replacement petrol. Check with your dealer/ manufacturer if you aren't sure, or check with an oil company's technical department if you're running an older motorcycle.

Catalytic converter

Leaded or lead-replacement fuel mustn't be used by a motorcycle fitted with a catalytic converter. Even one tankful can permanently damage the system.

Oil

The oil in your engine performs several tasks at high pressures and at temperatures up to 300°C. It helps to

- resist wear on moving surfaces

- combat the corrosive acids formed as the hydrocarbons in the fuel are burnt in the engine

- keep the engine cool.

You must keep the oil at the level recommended by the vehicle manufacturer. Check the oil level regularly and top it up when necessary, especially before a long journey. Make sure you always use the lubricants recommended in the vehicle handbook.

Over time, the oil will become contaminated with combustion products, metal particles and moisture. Regular oil and filter changes are necessary to ensure the engine is protected by clean oil.

How to check the oil level

Your motorcycle will have either

- a dipstick, or
- a sight glass

to show you the amount of oil in the engine. See your vehicle handbook for more information.

Checking the oil while the engine is cold will give a more accurate result. You should also make sure that the vehicle is on a level surface and upright. Use the centre stand if your motorcycle is fitted with one.

Motorcycles with a dipstick

Remove the dipstick and wipe it clean. Return it fully into the dipstick opening, then remove it again and look at the oil level. If the level is too low, top it up to the correct level using the manufacturer's recommended grade of oil.

Motorcycles with a sight glass

You may need a cloth to wipe the sight glass clean. The oil level should be between the 'max' and 'min' marks. If the level is too low, top it up to the correct level using the manufacturer's recommended grade of oil.

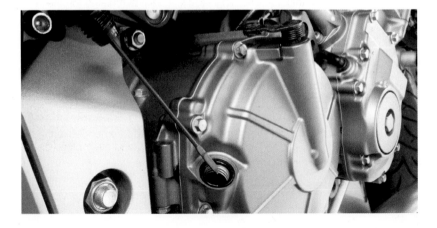

Oil changes

Observe the manufacturer's recommendations. If you make a large number of short journeys, especially in dusty conditions, change the oil more frequently. Remember to change the oil filter at the same time.

REMEMBER, oil is toxic and can cause skin problems. If you get it on your hands, wash it off immediately.

Keep containers storing oil out of the reach of children.

Oil use

The amount of oil an engine will use depends on the type of engine and the amount of wear, as well as how you ride.

You shouldn't

- run the engine when the oil level is below the minimum mark
- add so much oil that the level rises above the maximum mark. You'll create excess pressure, which could damage the engine seals and gaskets, and cause oil leaks.

Warning light

If the oil-pressure warning light on your instrument panel comes on when you're riding, stop as soon as you can and check the oil level.

Gearbox lubricating oils

Most motorcycles use the engine oil to lubricate the gearbox, but a few have a separate oil supply for this purpose. This oil is specially formulated for use in the gearbox. You should always follow the instructions in the vehicle handbook.

It isn't necessary to drain the gearbox in most cases, but the level should be checked at service intervals.

Shaft final drive lubricating oils

Motorcycles with a shaft final drive have a separate oil supply held in the final drive housing on the rear wheel hub.

There's a filler/level hole on the housing. Remember to stand the motorcycle upright when checking the final drive oil level.

It's important that the correct hypoid-type extreme-pressure oil specified in the vehicle handbook is used. You may have to squeeze in the top-up oil using a plastic bottle and tube.

Chain final drive lubricating oils

Final drive chains wear and require frequent lubrication and adjustment. Special motorcycle chain lubricants are available for this purpose. Allowing your drive chain to run dry will greatly increase the rate of wear.

The drive chain needs to be adjusted until the free play is as specified in the handbook. If the chain is worn or slack, it can jump off the sprocket and lock the rear wheel.

When you've adjusted the chain tension, you should check the rear wheel alignment. Marks may be provided beside the chain adjusters to make this easy.

Coolant

Many motorcycle engines are liquid-cooled, using a mixture of water and anti-freeze. This stays in the system all year round and helps to keep the engine comparatively cool while it's running. The anti-freeze stops the coolant from freezing in cold conditions.

The anti-freeze also contains a corrosion inhibitor, which reduces rust and prolongs the life of the system. In cold weather, maintain the recommended strength of anti-freeze. Have it checked at least annually – late summer or early autumn is best.

You should check the coolant level frequently, particularly before a long trip. Top it up with coolant as necessary. The need to top up often might indicate a leak or other fault in the cooling system; have it checked by your garage or dealer.

REMEMBER, never remove a radiator cap when the engine is hot, and never add cold water to an overheated engine.

Air filter

Replace the air filter at the intervals recommended by the manufacturer, or sooner if the vehicle is used in exceptionally dusty conditions.

⊙ Suspension, steering and wheels

Suspension

Several different types of suspension are fitted to motorcycles. These range from simple systems with no adjustment to sophisticated systems adjustable for

* preload
* compression
* rebound.

Some motorcycles have electronically adjustable suspension. Refer to your vehicle handbook for details.

Check your shock absorbers for oil leaks. A faulty seal will allow the damping oil to leak out and this can

* make the motorcycle difficult to control
* increase your stopping distance.

There's also a danger that oil leaking from the front forks or a faulty shock absorber may find its way onto the wheel, tyre and brake disc or drum.

Steering

Steering-head bearings

Steering-head bearings allow smooth steering movement. The bearings need to be checked for wear and correct adjustment. Badly adjusted or worn steering-head bearings can make the motorcycle difficult to control and may lead to weaving and wobbling.

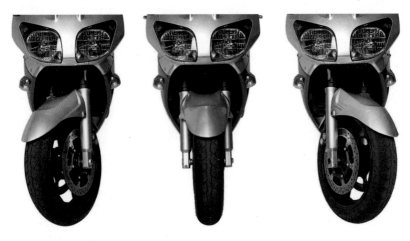

Movement

The handlebars should be free to move from full left lock to full right lock without

- any control cables being stretched, trapped or pinched
- any snagging between moving and fixed parts.

Wheels

Motorcycles may be fitted with

- spoked wheels
- alloy wheels
- pressed-steel wheels (small-wheeled machines only).

Check that the wheels are running 'true'. Spin each wheel in turn and watch where it passes a suspension arm or mudguard stay. If the wheel is buckled, this will show up.

Check spoked wheels for loose or broken spokes, and all wheels for cracks or visible damage. Regularly check wheel nuts and bolts for tightness.

Have your wheels balanced by an authorised dealer or tyre fitter.

Use the wheel-alignment marks to make sure the front and rear wheels are correctly aligned.

Wheel alignment

It's important for the rear wheel to be aligned precisely behind the front wheel. When adjusting the drive chain or refitting the rear wheel, it's possible to disturb the wheel alignment. Incorrectly aligned wheels can cause

- instability, especially when cornering
- increased tyre wear.

Many motorcycles have wheel-alignment marks stamped onto the frame by the chain adjusters. See your vehicle handbook for details.

Tyres

Tyre pressure

Keeping your tyres correctly inflated is vital for your safety. Incorrectly inflated tyres can cause

- loss of stability, affecting the steering
- reduced grip, affecting cornering and braking
- increased tyre wear
- increased fuel consumption.

Check your tyre pressures weekly, when the tyres are cold. The correct tyre pressures can be found in the vehicle handbook.

You might have to increase the pressure

- when carrying a pillion passenger
- when carrying a load
- when riding at sustained high speeds.

Tyre condition
In addition, you should check your tyres for

- tread depth and uneven tread wear
- cuts or splits
- small stones, glass or any other object stuck in the tyre
- grease or oil, which could affect the tyre's grip.

Excessive or uneven tyre wear can be caused by faults in the

- braking system
- suspension
- wheel alignment.

If you suspect a problem, have it checked by your garage.

Regulations
You mustn't use any tyre that has

- a cut longer than 25 mm or 10% of the width of the tyre, whichever is the greater, and which is deep enough to reach the ply
- a lump, bulge or tear caused by partial failure of its structure
- any exposed ply or cord
- been recut.

If there's any sign that the tyres have been damaged, they should be replaced.

Tread depth
Most tyres have tread-wear indicators. These are small raised mouldings in the bottom of the tread grooves, which are exposed when the tread is worn down to 1 mm. Some manufacturers design their tyres so that the wear indicators are exposed before the 1 mm minimum is reached. If you can see the wear indicators, use a tread-depth gauge to check how much tread remains.

> **FACTS** In order to stay legal, motorcycles with an engine size up to 50 cc must have tyres with an original, clearly visible groove pattern.
>
> For motorcycles over 50 cc, the legal minimum tyre-tread depth is 1 mm across 75% of the width of the tread, in a continuous band around the entire circumference. The remaining 25% should still have a visible tread pattern.

Motorcycles less than 50 cc

If your motorcycle has an engine capacity of less than 50 cc, the tyre tread may be less than 1 mm deep if the base of any groove that showed in the original tread can be seen clearly.

Punctures

If your machine suddenly becomes unstable, a puncture might be the cause. If this happens or a tyre bursts

- don't brake suddenly
- hold the handlebars firmly
- close the throttle to make the machine slow down
- try to keep a straight course
- stop gradually at the side of the road.

A punctured tyre should be properly repaired or replaced.

Replacing a tyre

When replacing a tyre, you should

- fit a tyre that's recommended by the manufacturer
- buy the correct type. Some machines require different types of tyre on the front and back wheels
- make sure the tyre is fitted to rotate in the direction of the tyre-rotation indicators.

Ride carefully on new tyres, until the shiny surface has worn off.

If you're replacing a rear tyre, make sure the new tyre is compatible with the one fitted to the front wheel.

⊙ Controls

Brakes

Two types of braking system are fitted to motorcycles: mechanically operated and hydraulically operated. With use, various parts of the braking system will wear and need adjustment or replacement.

Mechanically operated brakes

If your motorcycle has mechanically operated brakes

- periodic adjustment is necessary to compensate for stretching of the brake cables and for wear of the brake pads or shoes
- keep the pivots and cables lubricated to maintain their efficiency.

Hydraulically operated brakes

If your motorcycle has hydraulic brakes, check

- brake-fluid levels regularly
- couplings and joints for leaks
- flexible hoses for cuts or damage.

If your front brakes are badly worn, they'll become inefficient and you could damage the brake discs.

All braking systems

Brake pads and shoes gradually wear during use. Check and replace them as necessary.

For more information on braking, ABS and traction control, see section 5.

REMEMBER, anti-lock braking systems (ABS) will have a warning light. Generally, this will light up when you turn on the ignition and may not go out until the motorcycle is travelling at 5–10 mph (8–16 km/h).

Clutch

The clutch on your motorcycle may be

* cable operated

* hydraulically operated.

If your motorcycle has a cable-operated clutch, check

* the free play on the lever is as specified in the vehicle handbook

* it's correctly lubricated

* for fraying or chafing of the cable.

For motorcycles fitted with a hydraulically operated clutch, you should check the

- fluid level
- couplings and joints for leaks
- flexible hoses for cuts or damage.

Throttle

The throttle may have a single- or twin-cable arrangement. Check that the throttle

- operates smoothly
- closes fully when released.

Check that the cable

- isn't fraying or chafing
- isn't pulled when you turn the steering from lock to lock.

Some motorcycles have an electronically controlled throttle. This is known as a 'ride by wire'.

⊕ Electrical systems

Battery

Most modern batteries are maintenance-free and sealed for life. The terminals should be secure, clean and greased.

If the battery is fitted with a filler cap or caps, check the level of the fluid. The plates in each cell should be covered. Top up with distilled water if necessary, but avoid overfilling.

Lights

Check the operation of the front and rear lights, brake lights and indicators, including hazard warning lights if fitted, each time you use your motorcycle.

It's a good idea to carry a selection of spare bulbs and fuses. See your vehicle handbook for the bulb/fuse-replacement procedure.

Headlights must be properly adjusted to

*   avoid dazzling other road users
*   enable you to see the road ahead adequately.

All lights must be clean and in good working order, and show a steady light.

The horn

Check the horn is working properly and sounding clearly. Take care not to alarm or annoy others when doing so.

Indicators

If fitted, indicators must be clearly visible and in good working order. They must show the correct colour and flash between once and twice per second.

Section sixteen

⊙ Incidents, accidents and emergencies

This section covers

- The scene of an incident
- First aid on the road
- Fire and electric shock
- Tunnels

⊕ The scene of an incident

Arriving at the scene of an incident

If you're the first or among the first to arrive at the scene of an incident, avoid becoming a casualty yourself. Remember that

- further collisions can, and do, happen
- fire is a major hazard.

Warning other traffic
Do this by

- switching on hazard warning lights (if fitted) or other lights
- displaying an advance warning triangle (unless you're on a motorway)
- using any other means to warn other road users.

Switch off your engine and warn others to do the same. Put out cigarettes or other fire hazards and call the emergency services if necessary.

Calling the emergency services
Give full details of the location and casualties. On a motorway, this could mean going to the nearest emergency telephone.

Mobile phones
It can be very tempting to reach immediately for your mobile phone to call the emergency services.

Before you do, make sure you'll be able to tell them exactly where you are. This is particularly important on a motorway, where imprecise details can cause great problems for the emergency services. Location details are given on marker posts located on the hard shoulder. Always check these before you make your call.

Dealing with those involved
Move uninjured people away from the vehicles involved to a place of safety. On a motorway, this should be away from the carriageway, hard shoulder or central reservation.

Don't move casualties trapped in vehicles unless they're in danger. Be prepared to give first aid, as described later in this section.

Don't remove a motorcyclist's helmet unless it's essential to do so; for example, if they're having breathing difficulties.

When an ambulance arrives, give the crew as many facts as you can (but not assumptions, diagnoses, etc).

Incidents involving dangerous goods

If the incident involves a vehicle containing dangerous goods

* Switch off your engine and don't smoke.

* Keep well away from the vehicle.

* Call the emergency services and give the police or fire brigade as much information as possible about the labels and other markings. Don't use a mobile phone close to a vehicle carrying flammable loads.

* Beware of dangerous liquids, dust or vapours, no matter how small a concentration, or however minor the effects on you may seem.

Full details of hazard warning plates are given in The Highway Code.

Passing the scene of an incident

If you aren't one of the first to arrive at the scene of an incident, and enough people have already stopped to give assistance, you should continue past carefully and not be distracted by the incident.

If the incident is on the other side of a dual carriageway or motorway, don't slow down to look. You may cause another collision on your side of the road or, at the very least, additional and unnecessary traffic congestion.

Always give way to emergency and incident support vehicles. Watch out for their flashing lights and listen for their warning sirens. Depending on the type of vehicle, the flashing lights used could be red, blue, amber or green (see rules 106, 107, 219 and 281 in The Highway Code).

Police cones or vehicles

If these are obstructing the road, don't ride round them; you should stop. They mean that the road ahead is closed or blocked for an unspecified time.

If you're involved in a road traffic incident

You **MUST** stop. If there are injuries, either call an ambulance and the police yourself or ask someone else to do it. Ask them to return to you when they've made the call to confirm that they've made it.

You should

- give whatever help you can. People who seem to be unhurt may be suffering from shock and may, in fact, be unaware of their injuries
- ask yourself whether you're hurt too. If in doubt, get a check-up at the hospital.

If you hit a domestic or farm animal, try to find the owner to report any injuries.

For any incident involving

- injury to another person or animal
- damage to another vehicle or property

give your name and address, the name and address of the vehicle's owner and the registration number of the vehicle to anyone having reasonable grounds for requiring them. If this isn't possible at the time of the incident, you **MUST** report the incident to the police as soon as possible and in any case within 24 hours. In Northern Ireland you must do this immediately.

If there has been an injury, you must also give insurance details to the police. If you can't produce the insurance documents when you report the incident, you have up to seven days to produce them at a police station of your choice.

Witnesses
Note any witnesses and try to make sure they don't leave before you get their names and addresses.

Make a note of the numbers of any vehicles whose occupants might have witnessed the incident.

Other people involved in the incident
You'll need to exchange details and obtain

- other people's names, addresses and phone numbers
- the make(s) and registration number(s) of the other vehicle(s) involved
- insurance details.

Find out the vehicle owner's details too, if different.

Information

Gather as much information as you can, such as

- damage and/or injuries caused
- weather conditions
- road conditions
- details of other vehicles. Record all information: the colour, condition, whether the lights were on, and whether they were showing any indicator signals
- what was said by you and other people
- identification numbers of police involved
- any other possible factor in the incident.

Take photographs

If you have a camera or a mobile phone with a camera

- take pictures at the scene, including the registration plates of the vehicles involved
- try to record the conditions, vehicle damage and number of passengers present.

Some smartphone apps have a checklist feature designed to help you gather all the information you need in the event that you witness – or are involved in – a road traffic incident.

In gathering information, don't place yourself in any danger.

Draw a map

Show the situation before and after the incident, and give approximate distances

- between vehicles
- from road signs or junctions
- away from the kerb.

Note skid marks, where any witnesses were situated, street names, and vehicle speeds and directions.

Statements

If the police ask you for a statement, you don't have to make one straight away. It could be better to wait a while, even if you don't appear to be suffering from shock. Write your statement later. Take care with the wording, and keep a copy.

⊕ First aid on the road

The following information may be helpful, but there's no substitute for proper training. Any first aid given at the scene of an incident should be looked on only as a temporary measure until the emergency services arrive.

1. Deal with danger

Further collisions and fire are the main dangers following a crash. Approach any vehicle involved with care. Switch off all engines and, if possible, warn other traffic. Stop anyone from smoking.

2. Get help

Try to get the assistance of bystanders. Get someone to call the appropriate emergency services on 999 or 112 as soon as possible. The operator will need to know the exact location of the incident and the number of vehicles involved. Try to give information about the condition of any casualties; for example, if anyone is having difficulty breathing, is bleeding heavily or doesn't respond when spoken to.

3. Help those involved

Don't move casualties in vehicles unless there's the threat of further danger.

Don't remove a motorcyclist's helmet unless it's essential.

Don't give a casualty anything to eat or drink.

Try to make any casualty as warm and comfortable as you can. Protect them from rain or snow, but avoid unnecessary movement.

Give reassurance confidently and try not to leave a casualty alone or let them wander into the path of other traffic.

4. Provide emergency care

If someone is unconscious, follow the DR ABC code.		
Danger		Check for danger, such as approaching traffic, before you move towards the casualty.
Response		Ask the casualty questions and gently shake their shoulders to check for a response.
Airway		Check their airway is clear.
Breathing		Check for breathing for up to 10 seconds.
Compressions		**If the casualty isn't breathing** Place two hands in the centre of the chest and press down hard and fast – around 5–6 centimetres and about twice a second. You may only need to use one hand for a child and shouldn't press down as far.

If the casualty isn't breathing, consider giving mouth-to-mouth resuscitation.

		Check and, if necessary, clear their mouth and airway.
		Gently tilt their head back as far as possible.
		Pinch their nostrils together.
		Place your mouth over theirs. Give two breaths, each lasting one second. Continue with cycles of 30 chest compressions and two breaths until medical help arrives.

Unconscious and breathing

Don't move a casualty unless there's further danger. Movement could add to spinal or neck injury. If breathing stops, treat as recommended under 'DR ABC' above.

Don't attempt to remove a motorcyclist's helmet unless it's essential; for example, if the casualty isn't breathing normally. Otherwise, serious injury could result.

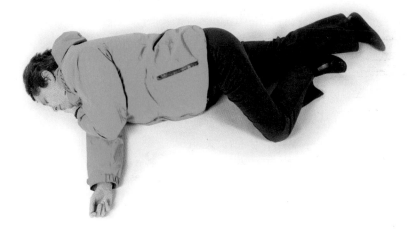

If an adult or child is unconscious and breathing, place them on their side in the recovery position (as shown above).

- Start with the casualty on their back and sit or crouch to one side of them.
- Place the arm nearest you straight out, at a right angle to their body.
- Roll them onto their side towards you.
- Turn the casualty's other arm palm upwards, and place this hand between the ground and the casualty's cheek.
- With your other hand, grasp the casualty's top leg just above the knee and pull it up at a right angle, keeping the foot on the ground. This will prevent them from rolling over any further.
- Make sure that the casualty's airway remains open and that you monitor their condition until medical help arrives.

Bleeding

First, check for anything that may be in the wound, such as glass. Taking care not to press on the object, build up padding on either side of it. If nothing is embedded, apply firm pressure over the wound to stem the flow of blood.

As soon as is practical, fasten a pad to the wound with a bandage or length of cloth. Use the cleanest material available.

If a limb is bleeding but not broken, raise it above the level of the heart to reduce the flow of blood. Be aware that any restriction of blood circulation for more than a short time could cause long-term injuries.

It's vital to obtain skilled medical help as soon as possible. Make sure that someone dials 999 or 112.

Dealing with shock

The effects of shock may not be immediately obvious. Warning signs to look for include

- paleness of the face (pallor)
- cold, clammy skin
- fast, shallow breathing
- fast, weak pulse
- yawning or sighing
- confusion
- loss of consciousness (in extreme cases).

Prompt treatment can help to deal with shock.

- Don't give the person anything to eat or drink. Their condition may be severe enough to require surgery, in which case it's better if the stomach is empty.
- Lay them down, with their head low and legs raised and supported, to increase the flow of blood to their head.
- Call 999 or 112 for medical help. Say that you think the person is in shock, and explain what you think caused it (such as bleeding or a heart attack).
- Loosen any tight clothing around the person's neck, chest and waist to make sure it doesn't constrict their blood flow.
- Fear and pain can make shock worse, by increasing the body's demand for oxygen, so, while you wait for help to arrive, it's important to keep the person comfortable, warm and calm. Do this by covering them with a coat or blanket and comforting and reassuring them.
- Keep checking their breathing, pulse and level of response.

- If they lose consciousness at any point, open their airway, check their breathing, and prepare to treat someone who has become unconscious.

Burns

Check the casualty for shock and, if possible, cool the burn for at least 10 minutes with plenty of clean, cold water or other non-toxic liquid. Don't try to remove anything that's sticking to the burn.

Be prepared

Always carry a first-aid kit – you might never need it, but it could save a life.

Learn first aid – you can get first-aid training from a qualified organisation such as St John Ambulance, St Andrew's First Aid, British Red Cross Society or any suitable qualified body. There are also first-aid courses targeted specifically at motorcyclists.

 Fire and electric shock

Fire

If you come across a vehicle fire, you may be able to help if the fire is small, you feel capable and suitable firefighting equipment is available. Otherwise, get everyone away from danger and make sure the emergency services are called.

Don't try to tackle a large fire, and don't take any risks.

In addition, while riding your motorcycle, it's important to be aware of the risk of fire. If you notice a strong smell of petrol, don't ignore it – stop and investigate.

Electric shock

Some incidents involve a vehicle hitting overhead cables or electrical supplies to traffic bollards, traffic lights or street lights. Check before trying to get someone out of a vehicle in such cases.

Don't touch any person who's obviously in contact with live electricity unless you can use some non-conducting item, such as a piece of dry wood, plastic or similar – anything wet shouldn't be used. You mustn't try to give first aid until electrical contact has been broken.

A person can also be electrocuted simply by being too close to a high-voltage overhead cable. Contact the provider (their telephone number may be shown on a nearby pole), then follow their advice.

⊛ Tunnels

If you break down or are involved in a road traffic incident in a tunnel

- Switch on your hazard warning lights (if fitted).
- Switch off the engine.
- Give first aid to any injured people, if you're able.
- Call for help from the nearest emergency point.

If your motorcycle is on fire

- Pull over to the side, switch off the engine and put the machine on its stand.
- Attempt to put out the fire using either an extinguisher carried on your motorcycle or the one available in the tunnel.
- Move without delay to an emergency exit if you can't put out the fire.
- Call for help from the nearest emergency point.

If the vehicle in front is on fire, switch on your hazard warning lights, then follow the above procedure, giving first aid to injured people if possible.

Some tunnels have signs with specific advice about what to do if you break down or are involved in an incident inside them. Make sure you follow these instructions and inform the tunnel controller of your location as soon as you can.

⊕ Ecosafe riding and the environment

This section covers

- What you can do
- Ecosafe riding
- Motorcycle maintenance

⊙ What you can do

Transport is an essential part of modern life, but we can't ignore its environmental consequences – local, regional and global. There's increasing public concern for the protection of our environment, with the result that many motor manufacturers are devoting more time, effort and resources to the development of environmentally friendly vehicles.

But you, as a rider, can also help. If you follow the principles of ecosafe riding set out in the following pages, you'll become a more environmentally friendly rider and

- your journeys will be more comfortable
- you could considerably reduce your fuel bills
- you could reduce those emissions that cause damage to the atmosphere.

In addition, you'll become a safer rider as you develop your planning, perception and anticipation skills to a high level.

Try to ride in an ecosafe manner at all times, whether you're riding for business or for pleasure. Fuel, like all forms of power, costs money as well as having an impact on the environment. Minimising the fuel or power you use is always important, both for the planet and for your pocket.

However, although it's good to save fuel, you mustn't compromise your own safety or that of other road users when attempting to do so. Road safety is more important than saving fuel. You should be prepared to adapt to changing conditions at all times, and it may be that you have to sacrifice fuel-saving for safety.

The effects of pollution

Air pollution contributes to health problems for many people. In densely populated areas, traffic is the biggest source of air pollution. Road transport accounts for a significant proportion of all emissions and the way we drive or ride can make a surprising difference to local air quality.

The particular problem with emissions from motor vehicles (including motorcycles) is that they're at ground level. People with conditions such as respiratory problems, heart disease or vascular disease are particularly exposed.

In addition, pollution from motor vehicles causes changes to communities and the landscape, including

* damage to vegetation
* deterioration and weakening of buildings and bridges
* the depletion of natural resources
* disruption of wildlife.

Fuel combustion produces

* carbon dioxide, a major greenhouse gas; transport accounts for about one-fifth of the carbon dioxide we produce in this country

Everyone has a responsibility to do what they can to safeguard the environment for future generations.

* nitric oxides; these add nitrogen to the atmosphere, causing damage and disturbance to the ecosystem.

Information about air pollution is available online at **http://uk-air.defra.gov.uk** and **www.gov.uk/defra**. You can also phone the free air pollution recorded information helpline on **0800 556 677**.

Catalytic converters
These are exhaust-treatment systems that remove up to 75% of carbon monoxide, nitrogen oxide and hydrocarbons.

The converter is a honeycomb-shaped filter with a total surface area about equal to a football pitch. This surface is coated with precious metals such as platinum, palladium and rhodium. These speed up a chemical reaction in the exhaust gases as the engine heats up. The oxygen content of the exhaust is monitored and a sensor triggers controls to adjust the air–fuel mixture.

The converter only deals with toxic and polluting gases. Carbon dioxide is still produced.

Leaded petrol can't be used in vehicles fitted with a catalytic converter. Even one tankful can permanently damage the system.

If you over-accelerate or exceed 3000 rpm, the catalytic converter can't clean up the emissions completely and will release some that are contaminated. Make sure, therefore, that you don't ride in such a way that this will occur.

What you can do to help

Motor vehicles have become a central feature in our lives, but it's still possible to use them in a manner that's less harmful to the environment by taking care and giving some thought to how, and when, we drive or ride.

We give some suggestions on the following pages about what you can do to help.

⊕ Ecosafe riding

Ecosafe riding is a recognised and proven style of riding that contributes to road safety while also reducing fuel consumption and emissions.

One of the main factors in increasing road safety is the emphasis on planning ahead so that you're prepared for potential hazards. Making this a feature of your riding will also mean that you use less fuel.

Hazard awareness and planning

You should be constantly scanning all around as you ride. Look into the far distance, middle distance and foreground, and also check behind and to the sides with frequent use of your mirrors.

Early recognition of potential hazards is important, but just looking isn't enough; you need to act correctly on what you've seen.

If you anticipate problems and take appropriate action to deal with hazards in plenty of time, you'll avoid

* late braking
* harsh acceleration.

Both of these actions lead to higher fuel consumption.

Keep a safe distance from the vehicle in front, as this will help you to plan your riding. Don't always use the brakes when the vehicle in front of you slows down. By just easing off the throttle, your motorcycle will slow down and fuel consumption will then be reduced.

If you plan early for hazards

* you'll avoid the need for sudden, harsh braking
* traffic will flow more smoothly
* you'll use less fuel.

Starting up and riding away

Avoid over-revving your engine when you start your motorcycle and pull away.

If your motorcycle is fitted with a manual choke and you need to use it to start the engine when it's cold, move the choke control to 'off' as soon as the engine will run smoothly without it.

Don't leave your engine running unnecessarily. If you're stationary and are likely to be so for more than a few minutes, you should switch off your engine to reduce emissions and noise pollution.

Choosing your speed

Keep within the speed limit
Always ride within the speed limit. Exceeding a speed limit by only a few miles per hour will mean that you use more fuel. More importantly, you'll also be breaking the law and increasing the risk of a collision.

Slow down

Motor vehicles travelling at 70 mph (112 km/h) use up to 30% more fuel to cover the same distance as those travelling at 50 mph (80 km/h). However, don't travel so slowly that you inconvenience other road users.

The throttle

Try to use the throttle smoothly and progressively. When appropriate, ease off the throttle and allow the momentum of the motorcycle to take you forward.

Wherever possible, avoid rapid acceleration or heavy braking, as this leads to greater fuel consumption and more pollution. Riding smoothly can reduce fuel consumption by about 15%, as well as reducing wear and tear on your machine.

Selecting gears

As soon as conditions allow, use the highest gear possible without making the engine struggle.

Check your fuel consumption

Check your fuel consumption regularly. To make sure you're getting the most from your machine, simply record the amount of fuel you put in against the number of miles travelled. This will help you to check whether you're using fuel efficiently.

If you haven't changed your method of riding, or the conditions in which you're riding, an increase in average fuel consumption may mean that you need to have your motorcycle serviced. An ecosafe rider is constantly aware of how much fuel their machine uses.

> If your motorcycle is fitted with a trip computer, it can help you check your fuel consumption.

Route planning

Avoid making unnecessary short journeys. When you do ride, plan your route and avoid known delays and roadworks. Always know where you're going – you'll use more fuel if you get lost.

Plan your journey beforehand.

- Use a map.
- Check a route planner on the internet.
- Program your satellite navigation (sat-nav) system, if you have one.
- Consider using an alternative route suggested by the sat-nav. This may add a few extra miles to your journey but can work out more fuel-efficient and less stressful.

More information about avoiding congestion can be found in section 18.

Off-road activities

If you take part in off-road activities, remember to

- avoid damaging fences, paths, grassland, etc
- take care not to harm livestock or wildlife
- respect the countryside in general
- ride in a responsible manner at all times.

➔ Motorcycle maintenance

Keeping your motorcycle well maintained is important to ensure maximum economy and the least damage to the environment.

You should make sure that your machine is serviced and maintained regularly.

- Make sure that the engine is tuned correctly. Badly tuned engines use more fuel and emit more exhaust fumes.

- Have your motorcycle serviced as recommended by the manufacturer. The cost of a service may well be less than the cost of running a badly maintained machine. For example, even slight brake drag can increase your fuel consumption.
- Make sure your garage includes an emissions check in the service.
- Make sure that your tyres are properly inflated. Incorrect tyre pressure results in shorter tyre life and may create a danger, as it can affect stability and stopping distance. Under-inflation can increase fuel consumption and emissions.
- If you do your own motorcycle maintenance, make sure that you send oil, old batteries and used tyres to a garage or local-authority site for recycling or safe disposal. Don't pour oil down the drain; it's illegal, harmful to the environment and could lead to prosecution.
- Use good-quality engine oil – if you use synthetic engine oil, rather than the cheaper mineral oil, you can save fuel.
- If you notice a strong smell of petrol at any time, check to find out where it's coming from. **Don't** use a naked flame near the motorcycle, and make sure that you have any fault fixed at the first opportunity.

Routine servicing ensures your engine is running at its most efficient and this keeps exhaust emissions to a minimum.

Section eighteen

⊙ Avoiding and dealing with congestion

This section covers

- Journey planning
- While riding
- Urban congestion

➡ Journey planning

The information available to the modern rider means that journey planning to avoid congestion can often be just a matter of checking online or using a satellite navigation (sat-nav) device.

Using this information can help you work out what time of day to travel, as well as whether there are any major route disruptions. It can also help you to schedule refuelling stops if you're travelling long distances.

Time of day

Much congestion is caused by work- and school-related travel. This causes delays in the early morning, late afternoon and early evening. If you don't have to travel at these times, try to avoid them. This will

- allow you to have an easier and more pleasant journey, and one that's less likely to be delayed
- ease traffic congestion.

Try to arrange appointments so that you avoid these times.

➡ While riding

Delays and diversions

Carry a map with you so that you can stop and check your position or identify an alternative route if you get held up or diverted.

If you're using a sat-nav system

- Your sat-nav won't always be correct, so take a hard-copy map with you in case of errors.

- You should always be aware that your sat-nav can be a distraction. Don't spend time looking at it when your attention should be focused on the road. If you're confused by any of its instructions, find a safe place to stop and review the route.

- Don't be distracted from making your own judgement about the safety of any manoeuvres.

- Before you turn, make sure you're allowed to do so by looking at any road signs.

Mobile phones

A mobile phone can be useful in the event of delays or breakdowns. If you need to make a call, find a safe place to stop first. If you're on a motorway, you'll either have to find a service area or leave the motorway.

Hazard perception

Looking well ahead to see what the traffic in front of you is doing will help you to plan your riding.

If you see the traffic ahead slowing down, ease off the throttle and slow down gradually, rather than leaving it late and having to brake harshly. If you slow down early, the traffic situation ahead may have cleared by the time you get there.

Constant speed

When you can see well ahead and the road conditions are good, you should travel at a steady speed. This is the time to use cruise control if it's fitted to your motorcycle.

Whether or not you have cruise control, choose a speed that's within the speed limit and one that you and your motorcycle can handle safely.

Make sure you also keep a safe distance from the vehicle in front. Remember to increase the gap on wet or icy roads. In foggy conditions, you'll have to slow down to a speed that allows you to stop within the distance you can see to be clear.

At busy times, some stretches of motorway have variable speed limits shown above the lanes. The speed limits shown on these signs are mandatory and appear on the gantries above the lanes to which they apply.

These speed limits are in place to allow traffic to travel at a constant speed. This has been shown to reduce 'bunching'. Keeping traffic at a constant speed over a longer distance has been shown to ease congestion.

Your overall journey time normally improves by keeping to a constant speed, even though at times it may appear that you could have travelled faster for shorter periods.

Lane discipline

Follow the normal rules relating to lane discipline (see section 11) to avoid holding up traffic behind you.

You mustn't normally ride on the hard shoulder of a motorway but, at roadworks and certain places where signs direct, the hard shoulder may become the left-hand lane.

Using sign information

Look well ahead for signals or signs, especially on a motorway. Signals situated on the central reservation apply to all lanes.

On very busy stretches, there may be overhead gantries with messages about congestion ahead and a separate sign for each lane. The messages may also give an alternative route, which you should use if at all possible.

If you aren't sure whether to use the alternative route (for example, whether you can reach your destination if you use the route suggested), take the next exit, pull over at the first available safe area (lay-by or service area) and look at a map.

On a motorway, once you've passed an exit and meet congestion, there may not be another chance to leave and you could be stuck in slow-moving or stationary traffic for some time. Take the opportunity to leave the motorway as soon as possible; you can always rejoin the motorway if you feel that's the best course of action once you've had time to consider the options.

If you need to change lanes to leave the motorway, do so in good time. At some junctions a lane may lead directly off the motorway. Only get in that lane if you wish to go in the direction indicated on the overhead signs.

Motorway signals can be used to warn you of a danger ahead. For example, there may be an incident, fog or a spillage that you're unable to see (see section 11).

Amber flashing lights warn of a hazard ahead. The signal may show

- a temporary maximum speed limit
- lanes that are closed
- a message such as 'Fog' or 'Queue'.

Adjust your speed and look out for the danger.

Don't increase your speed until you pass a signal that isn't flashing or one that gives the 'all clear' sign and you're sure it's safe to increase your speed.

⊕ Urban congestion

Congestion in urban areas leads to

* longer journey times
* frustration
* pollution through standing and slow-moving traffic.

London suffers the worst traffic congestion in the UK and amongst the worst in Europe. Various measures have been introduced to try to reduce the congestion and make traffic flow more freely. Red Routes and congestion charging are two of the schemes initiated in the London area. These are also being introduced into other congested towns and cities.

Transport strategy

A wide range of other measures have been designed to make public transport easier, cheaper, faster and more reliable.

If it isn't necessary to make your journey by motorcycle, you might want to consider alternative forms of transport.

For London, the Transport for London (TfL) journey planner (**tfl.gov.uk**) can help you discover the quickest and easiest routes for your journey using public transport. Alternatively, you can call TfL's Travel Information Call Centre on **0343 222 1234**.

Red Routes

Red Routes keep traffic moving and reduce the pollution that comes from vehicle emissions. Stopping and parking are allowed only within marked boxes.

Overnight and on Sundays, most controls are relaxed to allow unrestricted stopping.

There's a fixed penalty for an offence and illegally parked vehicles may be towed away.

There are five main types of Red Route markings.

Double red lines

Stopping isn't allowed at any time, for any reason. These lines are normally placed at road junctions or where parking or loading would be dangerous or cause serious congestion.

Single red lines

Parking, loading or picking up passengers isn't allowed during the day (generally 7.00 am to 7.00 pm). Stopping is allowed outside these hours and on Sundays.

Red boxes

These indicate that parking or loading is permitted at off-peak times during the day, normally from 10.00 am to 4.00 pm. Some boxes allow loading and some allow parking; the rules in each case are clearly shown on the sign.

White boxes

Parking or loading is allowed throughout the day, subject to restrictions shown on the sign.

Red Route clearway

There are no road markings, but clearway signs indicate that stopping isn't allowed at any time, apart from in marked lay-bys.

Congestion charging

Motorcycles are currently exempt from congestion charging.

Section nineteen
⊙ Riding abroad

This section covers

- Planning your journey
- Riding your own motorcycle abroad
- Hiring a motorcycle
- Riding in Europe
- Other things to consider

⊕ Planning your journey

Before you ride abroad, it's vital that you know the rules and practices related to driving in the country you're visiting. You'll need to consider

- riding rules and regulations, such as speed limits and which side of the road to ride on
- what documentation is needed for the country you're visiting
- whether you have the right insurance and breakdown cover
- equipment that you must carry by law.

You'll also need to decide whether to take your own motorcycle or hire one when you get there.

The major motoring organisations, the AA and RAC, can help you to organise and plan the details of your trip. They can

- save you time and money
- set up medical, travel and motorcycle insurance
- provide equipment for minor repairs and breakdowns
- help you organise the correct documents for your motorcycle or trailer.

You can often make your trip much easier by using their facilities and experience.

When planning a trip abroad, pay attention to all the details. You don't want to find you've forgotten something once you've left the UK.

For up-to-date advice to ensure that you comply with current rules/legislation when driving or riding abroad, visit this website.

www.gov.uk

Regulations

Speed limits

There are speed limits in all countries, but they vary from country to country. The motoring organisations provide a list of these various speed limits on their websites.

Make sure you know the limits for those countries you'll be travelling through. Many countries have severe on-the-spot fines for offenders, while others prosecute through the courts.

Alcohol and riding

Don't drink alcohol and ride. The laws and penalties abroad are often more severe than those in the UK.

Tunnels

Be aware that some tunnels in Europe can be several miles in length. Make sure you comply with any regulations that apply to them.

Plates

You need to display

- a nationality plate of the approved size and design at the rear of your motorcycle and any trailer you're towing
- a registration plate on your trailer, if you're towing one.

Documents

Insurance

Third-party motor-vehicle insurance is compulsory in most countries. Contact your insurer to make sure you're adequately covered.

Most insurance policies issued in the UK automatically provide third-party cover in EU member states and some other countries. They don't provide comprehensive cover unless you arrange this with your insurer, which may charge an extra premium.

Make sure you take the appropriate insurance certificate with you.

Your driving licence

You must carry your national driving licence when riding abroad. Even if you need an International Driving Permit (IDP), take your national licence too.

UK driving licences are generally accepted in other EU countries. However, if you still have an old-style paper licence, acceptance can't be guaranteed, so you may wish to update your licence before you travel. Alternatively, you can apply for an IDP.

If you want to ride a hired or borrowed motorcycle in the country you're visiting, ask about minimum age requirements in case they apply to you.

The hire company may also ask for a 'check code' so they can view your driving licence. You can find out how to get this code at **www.gov.uk/view-driving-licence**

International Driving Permit

Many non-EU countries still require an IDP. To qualify for one, you must be 18 or over.

To apply, you'll need

- your driving licence
- a passport-sized photograph
- a fee.

The major motoring organisations and the Post Office can issue your IDP.

Vehicle registration certificate

You must carry the original vehicle registration certificate with you.

If you don't have your vehicle registration certificate, apply to a vehicle registration office for a temporary certificate of registration (V379). Apply through your local post office well in advance of your journey.

If you plan to hire, borrow or lease a vehicle, you must ensure that you have all the relevant documents before you ride.

Passport/visa

All persons travelling must hold an up-to-date passport, valid for all countries through which they intend to travel. **Carry your passport(s) at all times.**

Keep a separate note of the number, date and place of issue of each passport, in case it's stolen or lost.

Travellers need a visa for some European countries. Check well in advance with the embassies or consulates concerned. This is particularly important if you hold a UK passport not issued in this country, or a passport from any other country.

Medical expenses insurance

You're strongly advised to take out comprehensive medical insurance for any trip abroad.

Most medical treatment can be obtained free of charge or at reduced cost from the healthcare schemes of countries with which the UK has reciprocal healthcare arrangements. However, you shouldn't rely on these arrangements alone.

European Health Insurance Card (EHIC)

This is issued free of charge and can be used to cover medical treatment for either an incident or illness within the European Economic Area (EEA).

The quickest and easiest way to get an EHIC is to apply online.

For more information, visit **nhs.uk/nhsengland/healthcareabroad**

You can also apply by phone on **0300 330 1350** or pick up an EHIC form from a post office.

Carnet de Passage

If you're planning to take your own vehicle outside Europe, you may need a Carnet de Passage. This is a customs document required in some countries to temporarily import a vehicle duty-free.

> To download an application form for a Carnet de Passage, visit this website.
>
> **rac.co.uk**

Equipment

In many countries, emergency equipment must be carried. Check with the motoring organisations to find out what's required in the countries you'll be visiting. This equipment may include the following.

Spare bulbs

Some countries require you to carry a spare set of bulbs in your vehicle.

Fluorescent vests

In some countries, such as France, the law requires motorists to either wear or carry with them a fluorescent vest. You should put this on before getting off your machine if you're involved in a breakdown or incident.

First-aid kit

Make sure you carry a first-aid kit. It's compulsory in some countries and strongly recommended in many others.

Breathalyser

In France, it's now compulsory for all motorists (except moped riders) to carry a breathalyser.

> As part of your planning, make a checklist of equipment, documents and other items you'll need. If you're travelling through several countries, check whether each item is compulsory or strongly recommended.

⊙ Riding your own motorcycle abroad

If you intend to ride your own motorcycle abroad, have it thoroughly checked and serviced before you travel. Checks to make include

- spare bulbs and fuses
- your toolkit: make sure all items are complete and in working order.

Also make sure you have a spare key.

Lights

Your lights may need to be altered for riding on the right. Deflectors are required in most countries. These prevent your dipped beam from dazzling drivers approaching on the left. Yellow-tinted headlights are no longer required in most countries.

Precautions against breakdown

Dealing with breakdowns abroad can be especially time-consuming and worrying without the help of one of the motoring organisations or breakdown services.

The best prevention is to have your motorcycle thoroughly serviced before you leave and to make regular checks along the way. Make sure you're prepared for minor breakdowns.

You must have all the necessary documents before leaving. Again, the motoring organisations will be able to tell you what's required in each country.

⊙ Hiring a motorcycle

If you choose to hire a motorcycle abroad, book in advance with a reputable firm. Booking in advance will allow you time to fully understand the terms of the agreement, the level of insurance cover, and any additional charges that might be incurred.

The hire company abroad may ask for a 'check code' so they can view your driving licence. You can find out how to get this code at **www.gov.uk/view-driving-licence**

As when riding your own motorcycle, it's vital that you understand the rules of the road and have all the necessary documentation for the areas you're visiting.

When you receive your motorcycle, make sure that

- you're familiar with the controls, and the motorcycle has all the essential equipment for the country you're in
- any existing damage on the motorcycle is noted
- you understand what the fuel requirements are (normally you'll be required to return the vehicle with either a full or empty tank – failure to comply with the specific requirements can be costly)
- you have the rental agreements in writing
- you're provided with information on what you need to do in the event of a breakdown or an incident.

> **REMEMBER**, hire motorcycles may be unfamiliar. Make sure that you understand the layout of the controls before you ride.

⊙ Riding in Europe

It can take you time to adjust to riding on the right.

When taking rear observation, remember that you must now look to the left, instead of to the right. This is vital – particularly before deciding to overtake.

Don't let your attention wander. It can be dangerous to forget where you are, even for a moment.

* Each time you set out, remember that you're in a foreign country where you must ride on the right.
* Take special care when you have to ride on the road again after a rest.

Avoid riding for long periods and don't ride when you're tired. You should also make sure that you avoid becoming dehydrated by stopping at regular intervals to drink water.

Defensive riding

Take extra care at roundabouts. Be aware of the possibility of changed priority.

Don't attempt to overtake until you're used to riding on the right.

Each time you move away, remember on which side of the road traffic will be approaching.

Make sure that you know the rules of the road; for example, in some countries you can turn right, with caution, at an amber filter light.

Motorway tolls

Find out about these. Include them in your budget and make sure that you carry an accepted method of payment. Frequent travellers may want to find out about the automated payment systems that are available in some countries.

⊕ Other things to consider

Planning your route

You can make your journey much easier by planning your route effectively. It's especially worth doing so when travelling abroad, where

* the roads are likely to be unfamiliar

- you may wish to avoid certain routes or roads
- you'd like to know the locations of tolls.

Most satellite navigation (sat-nav) systems can be used abroad, and motoring organisations can provide

- route guides
- summaries of motoring regulations
- details of tolls.

They'll also recommend alternative routes from continental ports or airports to specific destinations; for example, using motorways for speed and convenience or scenic routes for pleasure.

Security

Make sure any handbags, wallets or other valuables are safe and secure.

Never leave valuables unattended on your motorcycle overnight. Loss of possessions, passports, tickets, cash and credit cards can be distressing and inconvenient when you're abroad.

After your trip

Don't forget to adjust to riding on the left again as soon as you return.

⊕ Index

Learning to drive, ride or simply want to brush up on your knowledge?

The Official DVSA Learning Zone has launched with the car theory test module. This provides you with instant access to all the latest revision questions and answers on any internet connected device. Visit **www.dvsalearningzone.co.uk** Prices from £7.

SAVE 10% on official DVSA publications

Get ready to pass your theory and practical tests. Shop now at **www.safedrivingforlife.info/shop** and enter code SD10 to **SAVE 10%** or call **01603 696979** quoting SD10.*

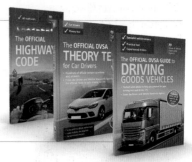

Revise on the go!

The Official DVSA Theory Test Kit for Car Drivers iPhone app

Designed to support the core Theory Test for Car Drivers learning material.

For everyone!

The Official DVSA Highway Code iPhone app

All the rules of the road at your fingertips.

 Available on the iPhone **App Store**

Check out the DVSA Safe Driving for Life Series of eBooks, which give you expert advice and tips on driving safely.

Visit **www.safedrivingforlife.info/shop/car/experienced**

Join the conversation safedrivinglife @safedrivinglife ▶ You Tube safedrivingforlifeinfo